THE HO

GW00889718

WINE

THE HOME LIBRARY

WINE

CHRISTOPHER FIELDEN

OCTOPUS BOOKS

CONTENTS

This edition published 1988 by
Octopus Books Limited
Michelin House
81 Fulham Road
London SW3 6RB

© Cathay Books 1984
ISBN 0 7064 3386 6

Printed in Hong Kong

INTRODUCTION

The past few years have seen a radical change in the eating and drinking habits of the average person in Britain. Travel abroad has been more readily available, eating out has become more common, and entertaining at home has also increased. All this has led to a rapid increase in the consumption of wine.

For every person who sniffs the wine in his glass, swirls it about and pontificates about it, there are 100,000 who drink it simply for pleasure, without thinking about it very much.

The aim of this book is to extend the knowledge of such people, so that they might experiment with different wines rather than stick to those they know. It will point out wines which might be similar in style, but rather better than those they drink. It will also try to clarify some of the apparent mysteries of what to the outsider appears a ritual.

There will be no technical details as to how each wine is produced, the date on which the grapes are picked, and so on. This may disappoint the wine-buff of long-standing, but he can find what he wants to know elsewhere. It will simply try to show the average wine-drinker how to interpret the label and what to expect from a particular bottle of wine.

The British may not be the greatest wine-drinkers in the world, but they must be the most cosmopolitan with such an extensive range of wines now available in wine stores and supermarkets. This book will attempt to introduce the major regions of wine-production and talk of the styles of wine they make.

If it gives the average wine-drinker a little more knowledge and shows them that wine is to be enjoyed but not worshipped, it will have achieved its aim.

WHAT IS WINE?

Nowadays, particularly in this country, wine has come to mean the fermented juice of any fruit, but more correctly it should be the fermented juice of the fruit of the vine—the grape—and it is only this that we shall discuss. In *'Le Savant du Foyer'*, a 19th-century French text book, there is a map showing where in the world the vine grew at that time: wild throughout the southern half of North America, much of South America and some of West Africa; for the production of wine in much of Europe, the west coast of South America and at the Cape of Good Hope; and for eating in North Africa, some of Arabia and much of Asia, including Japan.

Draining off a sample in a cellar in the Rheingau, Germany. The greatest hocks come from the vineyards in this region.

Today, three-quarters of the world's wine is made in Europe, but it is made in important quantities in North and South America, North and South Africa, Australia and, to a lesser extent, in New Zealand, Japan and China.

The vine needs fine summers and warm autumns to bring its fruit to maturity. It also needs a regular supply of water, though an excess of humidity is a dangerous enemy.

Vine-growing is concentrated in two belts: a substantial one in the northern hemisphere and a much less important one in the southern. The most northerly vineyard area is the Ahr Valley in West Germany and the most southerly is at Coonawarra in South Australia.

The grape is ideal for the production of an alcoholic drink because, when it is ripe, it is full of natural sugar. When fermented, this is converted into alcohol. The basic process of making wine is really quite simple: the grapes are pressed and the natural yeasts released from the skins get to work transforming the sugar in the juice into alcohol.

For red wines the skins are left with the juice to give the colour; for rosé wines they are taken away after a short time; and for white wines the juice is left to ferment without any skins at all.

Generally speaking, red and rosé wines are made from black grapes and white wines from white grapes, but this is not necessarily the case. The colouring matter in a grape normally lies in its skin, as you can see if you peel a black grape: the flesh is the same colour as that of a white grape. It is therefore possible to make a white wine from black grapes, by crushing them gently and taking the skins away immediately.

This is a very simple description of how wine is made. The quality of any wine, however, depends on several factors. Of these, two are provided by nature—the climate and the vineyard site—the rest by man. It has long been accepted that the best wines generally come from poor soil near the limits of where it is feasible to grow the wine. However, modern knowledge and experimentation, in such areas as California, have shown that great wines can be produced in areas that have long been considered unsuitable: nature can now be helped, even the climate can be changed.

A BRIEF A-Z OF GRAPE VARIETIES

As the study of wines is never-ending, so is that of grapes—the science even has its own name, *ampelography*. There must be several thousand species of grape around the world, ranging from those that still grow wild in parts of the eastern United States, to the new varieties being developed every year. The number of varieties used for making wine must also be in the thousands. Some varieties produce large quantities of inferior wine, others might give only minute quantities of high quality. It is up to the grower to decide what he wants to make, though in most of the traditional vineyard areas this has long since been decided for him.

In many regions the wine is made from several grape varieties whose products are blended together. There seems to be an increasing tendency, however, for wines to be made and sold under the name of a single grape variety. Such wines are called varietal wines.

The following are the 24 you are most likely to come across from among the countless horde producing wine around the world.

Aligoté (white). A variety seen in few places outside Burgundy, where it has its own appellation—the Bourgogne Aligoté. It is early ripening and makes wines rather low in tannin and alcohol, but somewhat high in acidity.

Cabernet Sauvignon (black). This is one of the great grapes of the world and is the predominant variety in the great vineyards of Bordeaux, particularly in the Médoc. It also makes outstanding wines in many of the new vineyard areas of the world including California, Australia, New Zealand,

Grape-picking with secateurs in Riquewihr, Alsace.

South America and Bulgaria. However, it has only a poor yield and is rather late to ripen and susceptible to disease. The wines are full of flavour and body.

Carignan (black, and sometimes white). Of Spanish origin, this is now the most widely planted variety in France. On the plain it has a large yield of rather dull wine, but is capable of making something rather better when planted on slopes. Probably at its best blended.

Chardonnay (white). Perhaps the most fashionable quality white variety in the world. In the last 20 years, its plantings have increased phenomenally in California. Probably best known as the base for all the great white Burgundies.

Chasselas (white). Mainly known as a table grape, it is little used for wine in France, except in Pouilly-sur-Loire and Alsace. Probably most widely planted in Switzerland, where it makes light wines under a number of names: the Perlan in Geneva, the Dorin in Vaud, and the Fendant in the Valais.

Surprisingly, Pinot Noir grapes are often used in Champagne.

White Gewürztraminer grapes ripen to a pinky colour.

Chenin Blanc (white). This grape is grown in the Loire Valley, particularly in Anjou and Touraine. Here in outstanding years, it makes the great sweet wines of Quarts de Chaume and Vouvray. It is also one of the most widely produced grapes in California.

Gamay (black, and occasionally white). This is the grape of the Beaujolais, where it makes light fruity wines, rather low in alcohol, but very agreeable to drink. It has since been planted in the Loire Valley, where it is sometimes used for making rosé wines. Two Gamays are grown in California: the Napa Gamay, which is now thought to have Beaujolais origins; and the Gamay Beaujolais, currently considered to be a member of the Pinot family.

Gewürztraminer (white). A grape which gives a very spicy, fruity wine. It probably originates from the Pfalz region of Germany, but gives its best wines in Alsace. It is also planted in the Alto-Adige in Italy, and in California and New Zealand, where the wines have the same characteristics, but to a less pronounced degree.

Merlot (black). This is the second great grape of Bordeaux, where it is generally blended with the Cabernet Sauvignon. It is the predominant variety in Saint Emilion and Pomerol. It is now being planted throughout the south of France, because it ripens early and makes supple (smooth), quick-maturing wines.

Müller-Thurgau (white). This is a cross between the Riesling and the Sylvaner grapes and has recently become one of the major varieties in Germany, because it can thrive in marginal climates and produces well. Its wines are normally sweet, but with a rather earthy background.

Muscat (white). There are at least two distinct families of Muscat grapes, but they both produce very richly flavoured, fruity wines. In the south of France they are generally sweet and high in strength; in Alsace they are bone dry.

Palomino (white). Wherever 'sherry-type' wines are made the Palomino grape is grown. It gives rather neutral wines, very low in acidity and thus liable to oxidize. It is the major variety in Jerez, and is also found in South Africa, Australia and California.

Pedro Ximenez (white). This is one of the important grapes of southern Spain. It is grown in Jerez, Montilla and Malaga especially to make the sweetening wine. It is probably related to the Riesling.

Pinot Blanc (white). This is often confused with the Chardonnay, but is a separate variety coming originally from Lorraine. In Alsace it is the Clevner and in Italy the Pinot Bianco. It gives a big yield of fruity, but slightly neutral wine. It is often used for making sparkling wines.

Pinot Gris (white). This has a variety of *noms de guerre*. In Alsace it is the Tokay; in Burgundy, the Pinot Beurot; in parts of the Loire Valley, the Malvoisie; in Germany, the Rulander; in Champagne, the Fromentot; and in Italy, the Pinot Grigio. Its wines are soft and appealing and low in acidity.

Pinot Noir (black). An early ripening, but very delicate variety that gives the great red wines of the Côte d'Or in Burgundy and is also widely planted in Champagne. In Germany it is known as the Blauburgunder, but does not make great wine. In California, it has the reputation of being a problem vine and few wineries have succeeded in equalling the best Burgundies with it.

Riesling (white). This name is abused wherever wine is made and there are a host of crypto-Rieslings on world markets. The true variety, the Rheinriesling, gives some of the greatest wines in the world. It is probably at its peak in

Germany, along the Mosel and in the Rheingau. It also makes the best wine in Alsace. It is capable of continuing to ripen throughout the autumn when it can take the noble rot (see page 22) and make outstanding sweet wines.

White wines from various European countries appear under such names as the Welsch Riesling, Laski Riesling, Olasz Riesling and Riesling Italico. These are not from the true Riesling, but lesser varieties, which still give good, if not great, easy-drinking wines.

Sangiovese (black). This is the main variety used in making Chianti, though it is also grown widely throughout northern Italy. It yields a small crop of lightly coloured wine, but with much finesse.

Sauvignon Blanc (white). This makes fine wines in the vineyards of Bordeaux and parts of the Loire Valley, notably Sancerre and Pouilly, where it gives full-flavoured, crisp wines. It is also widely found in California.

Sémillon (white). This grape reaches its peak in the south-west of France, particularly in the Bordeaux region, though it is being replaced to a certain extent by the Sauvignon. It makes excellent sweet wines, but is rather less successful for dry ones.

Sylvaner (white). Originally from Austria and widely planted in Germany and Alsace, the Sylvaner gives a high yield of rather neutral wine. The grapes are pleasant to eat.

Syrah (black). This variety takes its name from the city of Shiraz in Iran and is still known under this name in Australia, where it is widely planted. In France, it is the quality grape of the Rhône Valley, and is now being used to improve much of the wine of the Midi. It gives deep-coloured, full-bodied wines.

Tempranillo (black). This is one of Spain's great grapes and gives the quality to the red wines of Rioja and Navarra. It also appears in Penedès, under the name of Ull de Llebre, and in the Ribera del Duero as Tinto del Pais.

Zinfandel (black). The origins of this variety are obscure, but are now believed to be from Italy. It is widely planted in California, where it gives a robust, deep-flavoured wine. It can be 'late-harvested' and is often the base for the finer Californian 'ports'.

THE STYLE OF WINE

The quality of a wine also depends considerably on the various treatments the grower gives to his vines. Until the last few years, one of the biggest enemies of the red wine producer after a wet summer was mouldy grapes; there are now chemical sprays which minimize this danger. Sprays have also been developed over the years to combat other problems, such as insects or fungi, which plague the vines.

After the grape juice has fermented and turned into wine, its style will decide what will then happen to it. Some, and a prime example of this is Beaujolais Nouveau, will be bottled and drunk within a matter of weeks of the grapes being picked. Some will age for years in casks, before being bottled and left to improve still further for several more

Generally, pruning takes place in January and February. Here young vines are being pruned back to encourage new growth.

Modern production methods: the grapes are being discharged at the press house.

years. Some wines should not be drunk before they are 20 or more years old, though commercial considerations are lessening this number year by year; others have probably passed their peak when they are a year old.

Wine can be either sweet or dry, still or sparkling, low in strength or high. Most freshly pressed grape juice left to itself will in due course make a dry wine: all the sugar will be eaten up by the yeasts and converted into alcohol. However, in some vineyard areas in the best years, certain grapes—almost always white—will be so rich in natural sugar that the resultant wines become so high in alcohol that the ferments are killed off before they have consumed all the sugar. Such naturally sweet wines are produced in the Bordeaux region of Sauternes (see page 22), world-famous for its great sweet wines.

Sweet wines can be made by killing the yeasts, usually with sulphur, before they have finished their work, or by adding concentrated grape juice, which is naturally exceptionally sweet, to a completed wine. Both these methods can be dangerous in that apparently dead yeasts might come to life again in the bottle and start working on the sugar. This can give the wine an unwanted sparkle, a yeasty taste and a cloudy look.

Most wines ferment twice before they are complete. The first fermentation turns the sugar into alcohol. In the second, malic acids present in the wine, which have an appley taste, transform themselves into lactic acids, which are much less noticeable. Both these fermentations release gases which normally pass off into the air. However, if the second fermentation takes place when the wine is already bottled, the gas will be trapped in the bottle and you will have a sparkling wine (see page 54).

High-strength or fortified wines can be made in a variety of ways (see page 60). Port was discovered by chance in the late seventeenth century. The light wines of Portugal were very popular in England, as French wines were hard to come by in times of war. But the wines did not travel well and often arrived in England out of condition. To prevent this, one astute British shipper added a couple of gallons of brandy to each cask of wine before shipment to give it more body. His customers found this to be infinitely preferable in taste and wrote back asking for more. Thus was created one of the great fortified wines.

Within the world of wine then, there is an endless variety of styles, tastes and pleasures. A man who says he knows which wine he likes and is happy to stick with it is cutting himself off from a world of unending interest. Modern techniques, and increasing awareness on the part of the consumer, have ensured that the proportion of poor wine is ever declining; in a world where there is an excess of production over consumption, it is unlikely that poor wine will make its way in the market place for long.

TABLE WINES

In most countries producing fine wine, there is a regional hierarchy of grades of wine, with the production controls becoming more and more severe. Generally these controls cover the following: geographical—the wines can only come from certain vineyards and areas; grape variety—only certain types of grape may be grown; quantitative—only so many bottles per hectare may be produced; production techniques—the vines must be trained in a certain way and the wine vinified in a certain way; and strength—the wines must have a minimum degree of alcohol and, in a few rare cases, a maximum.

The vineyards of Château Ausone, where vines have been cultivated for 2,000 years.

It may seem that these controls are an effort on the part of the producer to make better wine, but that is too simple an answer. In some cases, these classifications have been introduced to restrict the quantity of wine produced in order to increase the price and give a better living to the grower.

Modern techniques mean that, in some cases, better wines can be made with other grapes, but the wines are not then entitled to the classification.

Finally, controls are only as good as the inspection system; the more complicated the controls, the more inspectors are needed. No country has, so far, developed an inspection system to match its controls.

Below are the various national classifications, in ascending order, beginning with the basic table wine. Even within a single country, there might be a vast difference in the quality of wines within the same classification. In some countries there are further classifications within a given wine region.

France: Vin de Table, Vin de Pays, Vin de Qualité Supérieure (V.D.Q.S.), Appellation Controlée (A.C.).

Germany: Deutscher Tafelwein, Qualitätswein bestimmte Anbaugebiete (QbA), Qualitätswein mit Prädikat (QmP).

Italy: Vino da Tavola, Denominazione di Origine Controllata (DOC), Denominazione di Origine Controllata Garantita (DOCG).

Spain: Vino de Mesa, Denominacion de Origen (DO).

FRANCE

There are few who would dispute that France has the greatest tradition of all wine-producing countries. For a long time it was also the country that produced the largest quantity of wine, but this is a claim that it can no longer

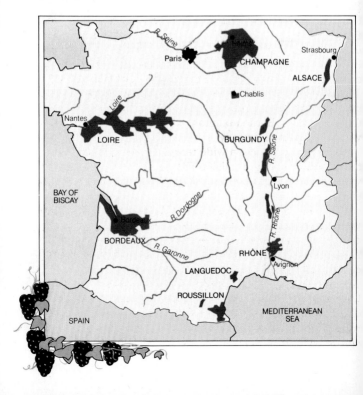

make, for Italy has now overtaken it in annual production.

If a line is drawn from Paris to the mouth of the river Loire, wine is widely produced in most of the area to the south. The wine varies in quality from some that is of such low quality that it is destined to be distilled; through the *vins ordinaires* sold in litre and plastic bottles; the small regional wines that are mainly consumed in the immediate area of their production; up to the great nobles of Bordeaux and Burgundy, which many of us will never have an opportunity of tasting because of their very rarity.

Wine consumption in France is falling, mainly at the lowest end of the market; young consumers particularly are asking for the better quality wines. The same is happening in many other countries and it is because of this that the prices of the finest wines are so high: their production is small, the demand is high, so prices rise. It is therefore in the medium ranges that the best value is to be found. This situation is accentuated by the fixed duty rates that we have in this country. On a £2.50 bottle of wine, perhaps only 20p has been paid to the producer; on a £3.50 bottle, he will have received five times as much.

WINE-PRODUCING REGIONS:
Bordeaux

I do not know whether it is for historical reasons that the British have always considered Bordeaux to produce the greatest wines of France, but it is certainly true to say that it is a region where there are much more clearly defined ideas of what is the perfect wine than in, for example, Burgundy. The scale of its production is much more grandiose than that of any of the other French regions producing quality wine. One château in Bordeaux might well produce as much as a whole village in Burgundy.

The region produces a wide range of red wines, for which the generic name in English is Claret. There is also an even wider choice of white wines ranging from bone-dry through the complete spectrum to very sweet.

There has long been a tradition in Bordeaux of selling wine under the name of the vineyard, which is generally described as a *château*. Whilst this might be a very stately home, it might just as well be an ordinary house, or even occasionally little more than a potting-shed!

The wine is generally made on the premises attached to the vineyard, though in some areas there are co-operative cellars where growers have grouped together to make their wine. Nearly all the better wines are now bottled at the *château* and the label will say *Mis en bouteille au château*.

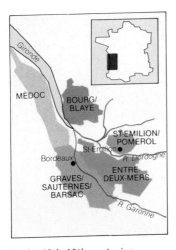

In the 12th-15th centuries, Bordeaux belonged to England.

The main merchants, who are largely grouped in the city of Bordeaux itself, will buy wines that have already been bottled, as well as wines in bulk, which they might bottle themselves under a *château* name or blend together with others and sell under a village or region name.

The vineyards of Bordeaux are in the south-west of France and have the rough shape of an inverted Y. The tail is the estuary of the Gironde and the two legs are the Garonne and Dordogne rivers. There are a number of grape varieties used, of which the best are the Cabernet Sauvignon and the Merlot for the red wines and the Sauvignon and the Sémillon for the whites.

Let us deal with the vineyard areas one by one, as identified in the map above.

THE MÉDOC This area stretches from a few miles north of Bordeaux to the Pointe de Graves, where the Gironde flows into the Atlantic Ocean. The soil of the area tends to be poor and sandy, but there are important minerals in it which determine the quality and flavour of the grapes. It is almost totally an area of red wine vineyards and there is a complicated hierarchy amongst the *châteaux*. The finest wines come from the southern half of the region, which is known as the Haut-Médoc. Within that area there are six villages which have the right to their own name as an *appellation contrôlée*. These are Pauillac, Saint Julien, Saint Estèphe, Margaux, Moulis and Listrac.

The hierarchy of the vineyards in the Médoc is based on a classification made as long ago as 1855. Whilst this has been criticized over the years, it has generally been accepted and there has only been one change made; Château Mouton-Rothschild was promoted from a second growth to a first growth by presidential decree in 1973. Of the wines classified into five groups in 1855, all but one (Haut-Brion from the Graves) came from the Haut-Médoc.

Since then there has been further classification of the lesser *châteaux* and we now have the following groups:

Classification	Chateau	Village
1er cru classé:	Ch. Lafite	Pauillac
	Ch. Latour	Pauillac
	Ch. Mouton-Rothschild	Pauillac
	Ch. Margaux	Margaux
2me cru classé:	14 châteaux – the best known are probably:	
	Ch. Léoville-Lascases	St. Julien
	Ch. Pichon Longueville Comtesse de Lalande	Pauillac
	Ch. Ducru-Beaucaillou	St. Julien
	Ch. Cos d'Estournel	St. Estèphe
3me cru classé:	14 châteaux	
4me cru classé:	10 châteaux	
5me cru classé:	18 châteaux	
Grand cru bourgeois exceptionnel:	19 châteaux	
Grand cru bourgeois:	44 châteaux	
Cru bourgeois:	60 châteaux	

Whilst it may not sound very flattering for a vineyard to be rated as 5th class, it is really one of the aristocrats amongst the thousands of Bordeaux vineyards—there are many vineyards which have not been even classified as *cru bourgeois*.

The dominant grape variety in the Médoc is the Cabernet Sauvignon. The wines are often full-bodied and tannic, with a rich deep fruit, and they need some age before reaching their peak. Generally speaking, the better the wine the longer it needs to age.

The wines of St. Estèphe are amongst the hardest in their youth, with those of Margaux and Saint Julien rather more soft and gracious. As can be seen from the classifications, the wines of Pauillac enjoy the highest reputation and are exceptionally well balanced.

GRAVES, SAUTERNES, BARSAC Just to the north of Bordeaux, on the left bank of the Garonne, begin the vineyards of the Graves. These often fight with the sprawling suburbs of the city for survival. Only the exceptional quality of some of them has saved them from having been turned into housing estates.

Whilst to the British mind Graves might primarily mean white wines ranging from dry to medium and, on the rare occasion, genuinely sweet, it in fact produces rather more red wine.

The area takes its name from the French word *graves*, which denotes a particular type of gravelly soil. It was also probably the first area in the region where vines were planted. (This would be logical as one would wish to have the vineyards as close to the city as possible.) A memory of the early vineyards is the name of one of the best wines of the Graves, *Château Pape-Clément*— Pope Clement V had a vineyard here at the beginning of the 14th century.

The best red wines are firm and rather tannic, whilst the lesser ones are pleasant, fruity clarets. The white wines are clean and dry, though rather soft. At the southern end of the area, where they are called *Graves supérieures*, they become distinctly sweet.

Sémillon grapes with noble rot which absorbs the liquid and leaves concentrated sugar.

In the 1855 classification of the vineyards of the Médoc (see page 20), one Graves vineyard, Château Haut-Brion, crept in at the highest level. The other vineyards were last classified in 1959. As a result, seven are entitled to call themselves *cru classé* on their labels for their red wines only, three, for their white wines only, and six for both their red and white wines.

Further still to the south come the vineyards of Sauternes, where the finest sweet white wine in the world is made. At vintage time the grapes are left on the vines and the misty autumnal mornings aid the development of a certain fungus (*botrytis cinerea*) on the skin of the grapes, known in France as the *pourriture noble* (noble rot, above). It absorbs all the water in the grapes, which shrivel up and then contain essence of sugar. The pickers pass through the vineyards three or four times over a period of weeks, picking only those grapes which are over-ripe. As there is so much sugar in the grapes, the yeasts are incapable of turning it all into alcohol and the wines have a lot of residual sweetness.

Five villages are entitled to call their wine Sauternes, but one of them, Barsac, can sell its wines under its own name if it wishes. The wines of Barsac tend to be rather less sweet.

Cérons, adjacent to Barsac, is a lesser appellation making sweet wines.

There is one *premier grand cru classé, Château d'Yquem*, and no one would dispute its right to this status; 11 *premiers crus classés*, of which the favourites in Britain might be *Châteaux Coutet* and *Climens*, both from Barsac; and 14 *deuxièmes crus*, some of which are not in production at present.

Naturally great Sauternes are expensive to make and, as demand for sweet wines has fallen over the years, it is not always rewarding to make the wine. As a result, many of the vineyards are being replanted to make red wines.

ENTRE DEUX MERS The area between the Dordogne and Garonne rivers is known as the Entre Deux Mers (between two seas). It is in these vineyards that much of the basic wine of Bordeaux is made, appearing on your table as the House Claret or under a brand name. Whilst Entre Deux Mers can be a red or white wine, in effect it is now almost all white, though a great deal of red is made and sold as Bordeaux.

One of the problems of this area over the past few years has been that the prices of the wine have been low, preventing the grower making much profit. In addition, balancing the supplies against the demand—at one time for red wine and at another for white—has been difficult; recently there has been an increase in the production of white wine.

Improvements in production techniques mean that a good Entre Deux Mers should be—and often is—very clean, fresh and crisp. It should be drunk young. Many wines are made solely from the Sauvignon grape and tend to have a fuller, fruity taste.

SAINT EMILION AND POMEROL On the north bank of the Dordogne, around the small town of Libourne, which used to be an important wine-port in its own right, lie the red wine vineyards of Saint Emilion and Pomerol. Many people find the wines of Bordeaux rather hard and unpleasant to drink—they should try the wines of these two regions. Here the Merlot grape plays a more dominant role, imparting some softness to the wines. Because of this some people compare the wines of Pomerol with those of Burgundy.

The vineyards of Saint Emilion can be divided into three areas: those on the plateau, those on the slopes and those on the plain. The best wines come from the first two categories. The two outstanding vineyards are Château Cheval Blanc and Château Ausone, which takes its name from the Roman poet and general, Ausonius, who is reputed to have owned a vineyard on the site.

The caves and vineyards of the ancient town of St-Emilion, at the heart of the St-Emilion district.

The classification in Saint Emilion takes into account possible fluctuations in the quality of the wines of a certain vineyard over the years and it is possible to be demoted. The two vineyards mentioned, and ten others, are *premiers grands crus classés*; another 60 or so are *grands crus classés*; and an unspecified number are just *grands crus*. For those seeking some quality guarantee it would seem that the word *classé* should appear on the label. In both Saint Emilion and Pomerol the properties tend to be smaller than elsewhere in Bordeaux and there can be much confusion over the similarity of names.

The satellite areas of Lussac, Montagne, Saint Georges, Puissegin and Parsac all add Saint Emilion to their name and offer lesser, but often enjoyable, easy-drinking red wines.

The total production of Pomerol is small, but it has the distinction of producing the most expensive of all clarets, *Château Pétrus*.

BOURG AND BLAYE From these two areas come some useful red and white wines which are rather soft and mature young. There are a host of small properties, some of which bottle and sell the wine themselves, but the majority sell their wine in bulk to the large Bordeaux merchants.

Burgundy

The vineyards of Burgundy lie roughly alongside the A6 motorway which runs from Paris to the Mediterranean. They begin near the town of Auxerre, about 100 miles south-east of Paris, where there is a pocket of vines producing the noted white wines of Chablis. There is then a gap of some 80 miles and the remaining vineyards stretch south from the town of Dijon to just north of Lyons. Generally the vines are on the final eastern-facing foothills of the Massif Central, on land too poor to produce anything else.

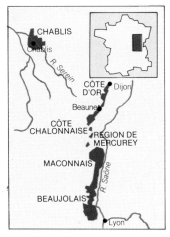

Traditionally, true Burgundy is made between Dijon and Côte Chalonnaise.

Four grape varieties predominate in Burgundy: for red wines, the Pinot Noir and the Gamay; for white wines, the Chardonnay and the Aligoté. In contrast to Bordeaux, the grapes are not generally blended together to make the wine—each has its individual, and solo, role.

Even though the production of the Burgundy vineyards is small, there is a multiplicity of names, ranging from some which are available for the whole area to some which are available for little more than an acre of vines. The following are just a few of them, starting at the bottom end of the scale.

Bourgogne Grand Ordinaire: this is often made from the lesser grape varieties from the poorer vineyards. Production is small and the wines, both red and white, are really only enjoyable in a good vintage. These wines are not often met.

Bourgogne Passetousgrains: this is a red wine which is made of a mixture of the Pinot and Gamay grapes. Traditionally, it was made by those growers who did not have enough vines to vinify the varieties separately. The wines tend to be rather acid when young, but soften out into an agreeable, but never great, bottle.

Bourgogne Aligoté: this is a white wine made from the Aligoté grape. It is normally higher in acidity and lower in alcohol than a wine made from the Chardonnay. It is the traditional base for the Burgundian aperitif *Kir*, which is a mixture of three-quarters white wine and one quarter *crème de cassis* (blackcurrant liqueur).

Bourgogne: whilst Bourgogne translates directly as Burgundy and therefore has a suggestion of being the basic wine of the area, this is not the case. It has to be made from the best grape varieties, suited to the particular area in which it is produced, and therefore has a certain quality. Given the complicated system of naming the wines in the region, this is often the Highest Common Factor of a blended wine and many good wines appear with this classification.

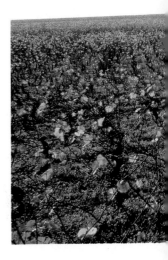

Starting at the north, the wine areas of Burgundy are as follows:

The famous Clos de Vougeot in the Côte de Nuits area of the Côte d'Or covers 124 acres.

CHABLIS Mostly white wines are made here, from the Chardonnay grape. The wines are all dry and should ideally be slightly 'flinty'. The total production is small, for this is one of the most northerly vineyard region of the world, and the worldwide reputation that it has built up is out of proportion to its availability.

There are eight vineyards, accounting for about five per cent of production, that have the right to call their wine *Chablis grand cru*. There are a further eleven vineyards, 40 per cent of production, with the status of *Chablis premier cru*. The rest of the wine is sold as Chablis. There are certain peripheral vineyards with the classification of *petit Chablis*. Whilst the finest *grand cru* wines should be drunk up to ten years old, most of the wines from the region are best at about two years old.

Traditionally Chablis is one of the driest wines of France, but recently, perhaps in order to have a broader appeal, the wines seem to be made in a rather less austere style. It is still a popular wine and is in demand all over the world.

From the same region, but only with the classification of a V.D.Q.S., comes *Sauvignon de Saint Bris*. This is a much fruitier wine, resembling perhaps a Sauvignon from Bordeaux or the Loire Valley.

CÔTE D'OR Here lies the heart of the quality vineyards of Burgundy, where both the greatest red and dry white wines are made. It is an area of small proprietors, whose holdings may be spread amongst several parcels of vines. Most of the growers will make the wine themselves, but then sell it in cask to the merchants, or *négociants* as they are known. These will blend wines from the area together to produce the necessary quantities of a given quality for the world markets. In Burgundy, it is helpful not just to know the name of the best vineyards and years, but also of the best merchants, as it is their name that will appear upon the label.

The classification of vineyards on the Côte d'Or is according to the potential quality of each plot of land. To complicate things, each vineyard might belong to a number of growers, each making his own wine and, in some cases, different parts of the same vineyard might have different classifications.

The magnificent 15th century Hospice de Beaune receives its income from the auction of new wine held here annually.

In the vineyard hierarchy of the Côte d'Or, the top wines are the *grands crus*. These can be recognized by the fact that they bear just the name of the vineyard, without the name of the village, e.g. *La Tâche*.

Next come the *premiers crus*, which have the name of the village, followed by the name of the vineyard in the same size type, e.g. *Puligny Montrachet Les Pucelles*.

Other vineyards, of lesser standing, appear in smaller type than the name of the village, e.g. *Savigny aux Fourches*.

One pitfall to beware of is the fact that at the turn of the century many villages added to the name of the village that of its best vineyard, in order to enhance the reputation of their wines. Thus the village of Gevrey took on Chambertin and became Gevrey-Chambertin. Now if you see *Gevrey-Chambertin* on a label, it is just a wine from the village; if you see *le Chambertin* it is from an outstanding *grand cru*.

The Côte d'Or vineyards fall into two halves. The northern part is known as the Côte de Nuits and is where the finest, full-bodied red wines come from. The village names to look out for, in geographical order, are: *Fixin, Gevrey-Chamber-*

tin, Morey Saint Denis, Chambolle-Musigny, Vougeot, Vosne-Romanée and Nuits-Saint-Georges. A wine called Côte de Nuits Villages is from one or more of a small number of villages of lesser standing, whilst Bourgogne Hautes Côtes de Nuits comes from the hinterland in the hills behind the better known vineyards.

The southern part of the Côte, known as the Côte de Beaune, is known for the best dry white wines in the world (even someone from Bordeaux might accept that) and some excellent red wines, which tend to be rather softer and quicker to reach their peak than those of the Côte de Nuits.

Look out for the following village names; those in brackets are rather less fashionable and therefore cheaper:

red: Aloxe-Corton, Beaune, Savigny, Pommard and Volnay. (Pernand-Vergelesses, Chorey les Beaune, Monthélie, Saint Aubin and Santenay.)

white: Aloxe-Corton, Meursault, Puligny-Montrachet and Chassagne-Montrachet. (Pernand-Vergelesses, Auxey-Duresses and Saint-Romain.)

A good, sound red wine should be a Côte de Beaune Villages, which will probably have been blended from several villages. Good, reasonably-priced wines can also be found as Bourgogne Hautes-Côtes de Beaune.

The red wines of the Côte d'Or, should be rich, soft and supple, with a good flavour of fruit, often reminiscent of blackcurrants or raspberries. The white wines will be dry, yet with a round, sometimes nutty taste.

RÉGION DE MERCUREY At the end of the Côte d'Or, there is a break with the narrow valley of the River Dheune and a group of vineyards known as the Region de Mercurey begins. Red and white wines are produced here, similar in style to those of the Côte d'Or but perhaps lacking some of the quality—and the price! The village names to look out for are Montagny and Rully for the best white wines, and Mercurey, Givry and Rully again for the best reds.

MÂCONNAIS This is the next group of vineyards moving southwards. From here come the best value for money white wines of Burgundy. For those who want a crisp dry wine I can particularly recommend those called Mâcon Blanc Villages, or those with Mâcon followed by the name of a village, such as Lugny, on the label. More expensive, but in the same style are Saint-Véran and Pouilly-Vinzelles.

Produced in a sun-trap amphitheatre of vines is the greatest wine of the area, Pouilly-Fuissé. This can be one of the strongest Burgundies and has a rich but still perfectly dry flavour. Because of competition, the *appellation 'Pouilly-Fuissé'* is now protected.

The Mâconnais also produces a number of sound but undistinguished red wines.

BEAUJOLAIS This is the final region of Burgundy. Here the grape variety is the Gamay and much of the wine is produced in modern co-operative cellars. This area is the source of between a half and two thirds of the total production of Burgundy. The wines, which are nearly all red, are made for hearty drinkers! They are soft and fruity and best served slightly chilled.

At the lowest level comes *Beaujolais*, a large proportion of which is now appearing as *Beaujolais Nouveau* shortly after the vintage. This traditionally comes on the market on November 15th and is the standard bearer for France's wines of the year. The Gamay gives a wine that matures quickly—as opposed to the longer-lived Pinot—and it is in the *Nouveau* that it best shows this ability. Another word you might see instead of *Nouveau* is *Primeûr*, which technically means that the wine has been bottled before December 15th, when the majority of the better wines of France are legally released on the market.

The next stage up in the hierarchy is *Beaujolais Villages*, whose wines will have rather more body. Above that come nine villages whose name appears on the label by itself. In approximate ascending order of fullness these are *Brouilly*, *Côte de Brouilly*, *Saint Amour*, *Juliénas*, *Fleurie*, *Chiroubles*, *Chénas*, and *Moulin-à-Vent*, which is the aristocrat of the Beaujolais as the wines are capable of maturing over a number of years.

Rhône
The vineyards of the Rhône lie down the valley of the river from the old Roman town of Vienne to the former papal city of Avignon. Both red and white wines are made, though the former predominate, and both tend to be full-bodied and rather rich. Whilst some of them can be drunk soon after the vintage—indeed a *Côtes du Rhône Nouveau* has now appeared in a bid to steal some of the Beaujolais market—the greatest are among the longest-lived wines from France.

A wide range of grape varieties is planted, each of them adding an ingredient to make a harmonious whole. The extreme example of this is at *Châteauneuf-du-Pape*, where up to thirteen species are commonly used in the blend.

These are some of the wines that you might come across. *Châteauneuf-du-Pape:* red and white, probably the best known name from the Rhône to the British consumer. Its vineyards are largely on very stony soil and they give red wines whose warmth is much suited to our damp climate. The white wines too are rather robust.

Coteaux du Tricastin: red, full bodied and grapey. Generally drunk rather young.

Coteaux du Vivarais: red, light and fruity, best drunk young.

Côte-Rôtie: red, from the northern Rhône. Full-bodied wines with a complex flavour. The vineyards are among the steepest anywhere in the world, the yield is small and the price is high.

Côtes du Rhône: red, white and rosé. The commonest wines of the region which, because of the vast number of possible sources, can vary widely in quality. The best reds, which are often bottled with a vineyard name, can be excellent. Generally speaking, Côtes du Rhône should be a safe name on any wine list.

Côtes du Rhône Villages: these come from the next rung up the ladder. Certain villages, such as Vacqueyras and Gigondas, because of their quality can now have their own name, by itself, on the label. Alternatively, both Côtes du Rhône and the name of an individual village, such as Beaumes de Venise, might appear. Such wines,

The Pont St. Benezet in Avignon, which is just south of the Châteauneuf-du-Pape vineyards.

which are always red, are very full bodied, with a deep
colour and a lot of flavour.

Côtes du Ventoux: red and a little white; slightly fuller in
body and rather soft.

Crozes-Hermitage: red and white. This region has a broad
range of qualities. The best wines, both red and white,
are grown on steep hillsides, but lesser wines come from
a plateau. At their best, the wines are deep and
long-lived, but some are now made for early maturation.
Generally they represent good value for money.

Hermitage: red and white. In Victorian times, the wines
from the steep hillside of Hermitage, overlooking the
River Rhône at Tain, were considered to be among the
greatest in the world. Somehow, their reputation has
been overtaken by those of other regions, but the wines
are still very complex and deep in flavour. In a
reasonable vintage, the red wines will continue impro-
ving for up to 40 years. The whites, too, age well, but not
on such a gigantic scale.

Lirac: red, rosé and white. The rosé wines are probably the
best from this region. They are high in alcohol, but soft
and deceptively easy to drink. The red wines can also
be good and reasonably priced.

Muscat de Beaumes de Venise: this is very sweet with a
pronounced flavour of the Muscat grape. It could
equally well appear in the fortified wine section.

Tavel: this is France's best rosé wine. It is full and fruity on
the nose, and clean and long in the mouth. It can be very
high in alcohol and when served chilled on a hot day
must be treated with respect.

Other more reasonably-priced red wines of quality can be
found under the names of *Cornas* and *Saint Joseph*. For the
drinker looking for a new taste in white wines, those of
Condrieu might appeal.

Loire

The Loire is the longest river in France and it produces a full
range of wines from its neighbouring vineyards. These
include very dry to very sweet white wines, fruity rosés,
fresh reds and some excellent sparkling wines. From the
area south of the city of Nantes, which lies near the mouth of
the river, come the wines named after the grape-variety
from which they are made, *Muscadet*. These are very dry
with a certain amount of acidity and a comparatively low
degree of alcohol. The best wines are said to come from the
Sèvre et Maine area, which will be on the label. A cheaper

At Tain in Hermitage, the vines grow on terraces built on the steep and stony hillside of the Rhône's east bank.

and rather coarser wine made in the same area, again named after its grape variety, is the *Gros Plant*.

From Anjou, further up the river, come a number of attractive rosé wines with a hint of sweetness; the best are made from the Cabernet grape. Among the white wines of this area come the excellent dry *Savennières* as well as a range of sweet wines from the very reasonably priced *Coteaux du Layon* to the honied and more expensive *Bonnezeaux* and *Quarts de Chaume*. Their sweetness comes in the same way as the wines of Sauternes (see page 22), so prices are not low. Saumur is known, too, for its fresh red wines and for its sparkling wines. The best of these are made by the *méthode champenoise* (see page 55).

Among the best red wines of the Loire, which are all fruity, slightly acid and made to be drunk young, are *Chinon* and *Bourgueil*, made from the Cabernet grape. There are also some enjoyable Beaujolais-style wines made from the Gamay grape, particularly in Touraine.

Also from Touraine come the great white wines of *Vouvray*, which can vary from bone-dry to richly sweet, according to the grower and vintage. Usually the label will give some idea of the style: *sec* meaning dry; *demi-sec*, medium-sweet; and *moelleux*, sweet.

Further still upstream are the vineyards of Sancerre, whose wines have become increasingly popular due to the closeness of Paris. Whilst enjoyable red and rosé wines are made, the true reputation of the area lies in its white wines, with their very full flavour so typical of the Sauvignon grape.

Alsace

Though Alsace is proud to be a part of France, it is prouder still to be itself and its atmosphere still maintains many traces of the times when it was under German rule. Whilst no one would describe the wines of Alsace as being Germanic in style, local viticulture has learnt how to absorb what is best, or most convenient, from its neighbours across the Rhine.

Three things are common in the vast majority of Alsatian wines: they are white, they are dry, and they are named after the grape variety from which they are made. They also tend to be classified, first of all, by the grape; if a variety is named on the label, you can assume that the wine is made 100 per cent from that variety.

One of the picturesque little Alsace villages, where almost everyone grows vines.

There are seven grapes commonly found on the label, the one of which the locals are proudest is the *Riesling*. This gives a dry wine, with a lot of body and crisp flavour. Next comes the *Gewürztraminer*. *Gewürz* is the German word for spicy, which describes the wine ideally. It has an intense, exotic flavour, particularly attractive to the newcomer to wine. The *Muscat* comes from the same family of grapes that give the muscatels around the world, but in Alsace the wine is dry and very grapey – difficult to match with any particular food. The *Pinot Gris* is more often called the *Tokay d'Alsace*, though it appears that the civil servants of Brussels are trying to ban this name so as to avoid any confusion with the Tokay wine of Hungary. A dry wine, it is nevertheless very rich and soft—and high in alcohol.

The lesser grapes are the Clevner or Pinot Blanc, which makes a plain, but rather fruity wine; the Sylvaner, with a hint more class; and the Pinot Noir, which gives what the Alsatians describe as a red wine, but which more often is a fullish rosé.

Wines made from any other grape variety, or a blend of grapes, may be called *Edelzwicker*, but more often appear under a brand name. Vineyard names are rare in Alsace, but a new classification of *grand cru* is coming into effect, which will be attached to certain specified sites.

More common as a means of classification is one that is individual to each grower or merchant, such as *réserve personelle* or *sélection . . .* These have no legal backing and their importance depends on the standing of the producer. Alsace has thousands of small producers, but generally only the wines of the better ones find their way to Britain.

On the wines of Alsace one often comes across medals from various wine fairs, which have a variety of reputations. Probably the most valuable medal is one from the Concours Agricole in Paris, followed by the National Wine Fair in Mâcon and the regional fair in Colmar. Also of significance is the seal of the Confrérie Saint Etienne.

I have said that Alsace wines are dry. Over the past few years, two official designations of quality have appeared: *Vendange Tardive* and *Sélection de Grains Nobles*. The first means late-picked and the latter, individual selection of super-ripened grapes. Such wines are only made in the very best years and are respectively, sweet and very sweet.

Some growers feel that such wines are nothing less than copies of the German *Spätlese* and *Beerenauslese* wines and so refuse to make them, or else make them as very powerful but dry wines. Unfortunately, there is no way of telling from the label what the wine will taste like—again, you just have to know the producer.

Loading-up the grapes in an Alsace vineyard.

The rest of France

Wine is made widely in France, yet much of it is never seen abroad, either because it is made in such small quantities that it is largely drunk in the area where it is made, or else because it is just not good enough—and probably destined for distillation.

Much of this latter wine has traditionally been made in the south of France, particularly in the area between the mouth of the river Rhône and the Pyrenees. Here there is a seemingly endless sea of vines, and in this sea there are certain areas and growers where special efforts are being made to produce better wine. Nearly all of it is red, full-bodied and robust.

Some of the best wines will have been aged in oak to soften them and in some cases, grape varieties such as the Cabernet Sauvignon, the Merlot and the Syrah, which are foreign to the region, will have been imported to improve the blend.

Single vineyard names are also becoming more frequent and whilst it is not always true, it might be said that if someone is proud enough to put the name of his property on a wine, it should be worthy of bearing that name.

Among the regional names, the most common are *Côtes du Roussillon, Costières du Gard, Minervois, Corbières* and *Fitou.* There are also many good *Vins de Pays* being made. One of the best of these comes from the Tarn Valley, between the Midi and Bordeaux. There too is made a good white wine, *Gaillac.*

Between the mouth of the Rhône and the Italian border good red and white wines are made at Bandol and Cassis. From the other vineyards of Provence, the rosé wines have the best reputation. They and the reds are at their best chilled and drunk under a summer sun on a pavement café watching all the attractions of the Riviera pass by.

Similarly, the wines of Savoie are 'tourist' wines, drunk in the ski resorts. The best are crisp white wines, often with a slight bubble to them. *Crépy* is a name to look for, though because production is small, its price is often higher than its value.

Further north in the Juras, some interesting wines are made around the town of Arbois. A local speciality is their rosé wine, which is considered by many to be the second best in France—after *Tavel*. More interesting is the *vin jaune*, which is a natural wine rather like a *fino* sherry. It seems to age indefinitely. The best comes from the village of Château Châlon.

To the east of the Bordeaux vineyards lie those of Bergerac, where good dry, and sometimes sweeter, white wines are made, as well as some very sound reds. The best sweet wines come from the area of Monbazillac and dry whites from Montravel.

If you are in France, it is always worthwhile trying the local wine. Often it will be cheap. Occasionally it might be a disaster! But asking for it can be a useful way of 'getting in' with the locals!

GERMANY

Whilst the reputation of German wines is enormous, the production is quite small. Germans tend to drink them on their own, not with food, for they are often sweet and generally low in alcohol.

There are basic quality levels in the wines of Germany (see page 18) and at the highest of these, QmP, there are several words used to describe the style of the wine. In ascending order of potential alcohol and therefore, in this country, of sweetness, come *Kabinett, Spätlese, Auslese, Beerenauslese,* and *Trockenbeerenauslese,* which can only be made in the best years; they last for a very long time and, because only minute quantities are made, they are very expensive indeed.

Trockenbeerenauslese should not be confused with *Trocken,* which means dry. More and more German wines are being made in this style.

Another rarity is *Eiswein,* made from ripe grapes which have been frozen while still on the vine. They must be picked in a temperature below −6°C (26°F), when the water in the grapes is frozen and only the sugar remains in a liquid state. The resulting wines are high in acidity and expensive.

Neat, orderly vineyards just south of Bacharach in the Rhine Valley.
Nearly all the wines produced along the Rhine are white.

Much more common in British shops, and from the other end of the scale, is *Liebfraumilch*. Originally this was made just in a small vineyard in the town of Worms, but now it is generally a soft, pleasant blended wine, of largely indeterminate source. *Moselbluemchen* is a similar quality but comes specifically from the Mosel valley.

A German wine label must show its quality category, the region it has come from and the name of the producer. The name of the village and vineyard, the grape variety and the vintage are also often shown.

While Germany does make some red and rosé wine, these are not often found in Britain, so we will concentrate on the white wines. For these, the main grape varieties are the Riesling, the Sylvaner and the Müller-Thurgau. The finest wines are made with the Riesling; those from the Sylvaner tend to be rather soft; the Müller-Thurgau are light with a hard background. Between them, these three types of grapes account for approximately three-quarters of the wine production of Germany.

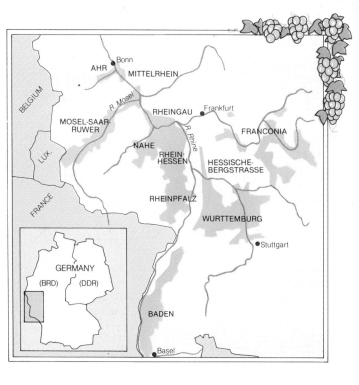

WINE-PRODUCING REGIONS:
Rheinpfalz
This area is also known as the Palatinate and the vineyards are a northern continuation of those of Alsace. This is Germany's most important vineyard area but much of the wine is of inferior quality. The best are rich and luscious, though some find them lacking in finesse. The village names to look out for include Deidesheim, Forst, Wachenheim and Ruppertsberg.

Rheinhessen
These vineyards are on the left bank of the Rhine. The wines are generally soft and undistinguished, coming from the Sylvaner and Müller-Thurgau grapes.
Villages: Nierstein, Oppenheim.

Nahe
The Nahe is a tributary of the Rhine. Its best wines are made from the Riesling—they are very clean and agreeable.
Villages: Schlossböckelheim, Bad Kreuznach.

Mittelrhein
These are the most northerly vineyards in the valley of the Rhine itself, stretching south-east from Bonn. Their wines are mainly drunk in the immediate neighbourhood.

Mosel, Saar and Ruwer
The vineyards of the Mosel and its tributaries produce wonderfully delicate wines from the Riesling grape. The best are on the steep, slatey slopes on either side of the serpentine river. A refreshing light acidity adds to the graceful charm of the finer wines.
Villages: *Mosel*: Bernkastel, Piesport, Trittenheim, Graach, Wehlen, Zeltingen.
Saar: Wiltingen, Serrig.
Ruwer: Kasel, Waldrach.

Rheingau
From this short stretch of villages on the right bank of the Rhine come the greatest hocks. Here the vineyards face due south and the climate is ideal for making late-picked wines from the Riesling.
Villages: Rüdesheim, Winkel, Oestrich, Hattenheim, Eltville, Erbach.

Hessische-Bergstrasse
This is a minor area of vineyards; the region is also

The village of Bernkastel seen from the Doktor vineyards which overlook the river Mosel.

well-known for its orchards. The wines are rather light and quick to mature. They are almost unknown in Britain.

Baden
These are the most southerly of Germany's vineyards, with the best wines coming from the volcanic outcrop of the Kaiserstühl. The main grape varieties used are the full-bodied Rülander (Pinot Gris) for white wines and the Spätburgunder (Pinot Noir) for red wines.

Wurttemberg
A wide range of grape varieties is used to produce a broad range of wines, few of which ever reach this country. More red wine than white is made and much of it is of very indifferent quality.

Franconia
It is from here that *steinwein* comes in its flask-shaped bottle, the *bocksbeutel*. The vineyards are steep, and full-bodied and often rather austere wines are made. The best come from around the town of Würzburg.

Ahr
This pleasant little valley is noted for two things: its vineyards are the most northerly in Europe and it makes what is supposed to be Germany's best red wine, some of which is turned into sparkling wine. Again, these are very rarely found in Britain.

ITALY

Italy is now the greatest wine-producing country. Although a wine law was introduced in 1963, the system appears almost anarchic as every village appears to have its own controlled name with its particular legislation. To complicate things even more, some of the more forward-looking growers have begun to use methods or grape varieties not traditional to their area and thus make wines which can only be called *vino di tavola*, though they are, in fact, of far superior quality.

The name of an Italian wine might be a grape variety, a region, or a style of wine, and often a combination of these. This breakdown of some of the commoner names might make things simpler.

Aglianico: a black grape making full-bodied red wines. The best probably come from Vulture, in the instep of Italy.

Albana: a white grape for dry and not-so-dry wines. High in alcohol. Albana di Romagna is a regular favourite.

Alto Adige: an area in the north of Italy, formerly belonging to Austria, where many of Italy's most interesting wines are produced, often from French grape-varieties. The labelling is in a German style.

Amarone: a wine from Valpolicella in Veneto, which is fuller-bodied and has received extra ageing.

Barbaresco: full, meaty red wine from Piedmont in the north-west of Italy. Generally drunk when three or four years old.

Barbera: a black grape used widely in Piedmont. Deep in colour and high in alcohol.

Bardolino: a light fresh red wine, best drunk young and slightly chilled. Made on the shores of Lake Garda. *Chiaretto di Bardolino* is a light dry rosé.

Barolo: one of Italy's great red wines. Full of body and colour; ages well. Made from the Nebbiolo grape in Piedmont.

Brunello: a black grape, related to the Sangiovese. Its best wine comes from Montalcino in Tuscany. This needs to age well before drinking, and the bottle needs to be opened in advance to show at its best.

Cabernet: the great Bordeaux grape now being introduced in Italy, notably in the Alto Adige, and in the Chianti region.

Carmignano: a Chianti-style wine, made in the region of Florence.

Castelli Romani: a region close to Rome making simple, dry and slightly sweet white wines.

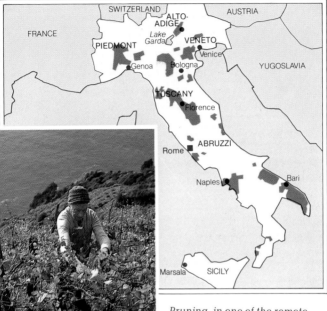

Pruning, in one of the remote Cinque Terre vineyards.

Chianti: perhaps the most over-exposed wine in Italy, from Tuscany. The better wines, which often come from the Chianti Classico area and can have a black cockerel on the neck label, appear in a Bordeaux-shaped bottle. The lesser quality wines come in wicker-covered flasks.

Chiaretto del Garda: a light-coloured, bright red wine from the shores of Lake Garda, ideal for summer drinking.

Cinque Terre: fine dry white wines made in five remote villages along the coast from Genoa.

Dolcetto: a black grape making light, fruity wines in the Beaujolais style, mainly in Piedmont.

Est! Est Est!: a dry, or sometimes slightly sweet, white wine produced north of Rome.

Frascati: a honey-coloured wine from near Rome. It has a very pleasant taste and can be dry or medium sweet.

Gattinara: a red wine from the Nebbiolo grape, made in the hills around Novara in Piedmont. It is at its best at about ten years old, when it is soft and full-bodied.

Grignolino: a black grape from Piedmont which gives light easy-to-drink wines.

Lambrusco (DOC): the *succés fou* of the Italian wine trade. A rather commercial slightly sweet, slightly sparkling red wine made near Bologna.

Malvasia: a family of white grapes, growing widely in southern Italy. When it appears on a wine label, it is generally a sweet dessert wine.

Merlot: another Bordeaux grape variety, now being used to improve the quality of red wines.

Montepulciano: a traditional black grape probably at its best in the Abruzzi. Its best wine is sold as *Cerasuola*.

Moscato: the Muscat grape producing a range of sweet, often sparkling wines.

Nebbiolo: one of the great black grapes of Piedmont. Its wines generally need some ageing to soften.

Orvieto: a white wine made round the town of the same name some 60 miles north of Rome. It comes in dry and medium styles.

Picolit: a sweet and expensive white wine made near the Yugoslav frontier. Once one of the great wines of Europe.

Pinot Grigio: the Pinot Gris of France. In Italy it makes sound, rather alcoholic, agreeable white wines.

Prosecco: a white grape grown north of Venice, which makes slightly sweet wines, both still and sparkling.

Raboso: a black grape found in the Veneto region, where it makes an agreeable, everyday wine.

Recioto: this wine is made by picking bunches of grapes and leaving them to hang under cover to concentrate the sugar content. The result is a sweet, heavy wine.

Sangiovese: a black grape used in Chianti and elsewhere. By itself it gives a full-bodied wine that ages well.

Soave: the soundest, safest white wine in Italy. It is never likely to offend but rarely thrills. Very pale in colour.

Spanna: this is the local name in Piedmont for the Nebbiolo grape, whose name often appears on labels.

Terlano: this is the centre of the Alto Adige wine region where German is the language spoken and the wine labels are in Germanic style.

Torgiano: a small area between Rome and Florence. The reds have some of the softness of a Saint Emilion and the whites are clean and dry.

Trebbiano: a white grape which gives, by itself, sound but rarely distinguished wines.

Valpolicella: one of the standard red wines of Italy, made between Venice and Lake Garda.

Verdicchio: a white grape giving rather nutty-tasting wines, with a pale straw colour.

Certain words are used to show the higher status of certain wines. *Riserva* suggests that it has been aged longer; *superiore* that it is probably higher in alcohol; and *classico* that it comes from the traditional centre of the vineyard area.

SPAIN

If Italy now produces the largest amount of wine in the world, Spain has the greatest area under vines. The old traditions of viticulture and vinification have been slow to change, so the production per acre is often small and the quality undistinguished. However, great strides have been made over the past few years and the future is looking bright for those wineries prepared to experiment.

Because of its stable climate, Spain has many advantages in the making of wine, but the tastes of the Spaniards themselves have not always had international appeal. The red wines have often been over-high in alcohol and aged too long in oak, whilst the whites have been oxidized and flabby, through lack of balancing acidity. Spain has a lot of potential and great wines are now being made in the finest regions.

WINE-PRODUCING REGIONS:
Rioja

Traditionally the wines of Rioja have been the greatest in Spain. When the louse *phylloxera vastatrix* devastated the vineyards of Bordeaux towards the end of the last century, many of the growers crossed the Pyrenees and settled in the upper valley of the Ebro in north-west Spain.

Vines planted in small plots in the Rioja region.

The red wines are made from the Tempranillo, Graciano, Mazuelo and Garnacha grapes and the white wines from the Viura, Malvasia and white Garnacha.

There are three distinct vineyard areas in the region: the Rioja Alta, where the finest wines are made; the Rioja Alavesa, whose wines have more finesse and delicacy; and the Rioja Baja, where the dominant grape variety is the Garnacha, giving wines high in alcohol and short-lived. Many companies blend wines from the three areas to achieve the perfect balance.

Ageing in casks gives Spanish wines their woody flavour.

Traditionally, the wines—both red and white—have been aged in cask for long periods and only bottled shortly before consumption; this has given them a pronounced woody taste, which appeals to some. Recently however there has been a move towards ageing the reds in cask for eighteen months or two years and then bottling them, making softer wine in the Bordeaux style. The white wines in some *bodegas* are now fermented out at low temperature and bottled without ever seeing a cask. This gives them an agreeable fruity flavour.

A wine that is described as *reserva*, should have aged in cask for a minimum of two years, followed by a further year in bottle. A *gran reserva* will have spent at least three years in an oak cask and another year in bottle.

Penedés

This is perhaps the easiest of all the Spanish wine regions for the tourist to visit, for it lies behind the coast to the south of Barcelona. Red wines are made where it is hotter, nearer to the sea. They are generally rather soft and should not be drunk more than three or four years old. The white wines, which come from the cooler vineyards in the hills, can be of exceptional quality and certain growers have experimented, successfully, with such French varieties as the Chardonnay and the German Gewürztraminer variety. The same growers are also making fuller-bodied, longer-lasting red wines from the Cabernet Sauvignon and the Pinot Noir. Because of the comparative coolness of its climate, Penedés has probably the best opportunity of making quality wines in Spain. It is also the centre of the Spanish sparkling wine trade.

Navarra

The vineyards of Navarra adjoin, and even overlap, those of Rioja. Historically, however, they have not had the same reputation. The region has been known for its powerful rosé wines, with an overbearing degree of alcohol. These are now being replaced by red and white wines, often in the same style as those of Rioja. The most successful companies are those who have adopted new techniques of vinification.

Valdepeñas

From here come the best wines of La Mancha, in the centre of Spain, to the south of Madrid. The white wines are often rather drab and lacking in balancing acidity, although efforts are being made to pick the grapes earlier so that fresher wines can be made. The red wines, with their refreshingly fruity characteristics, are more agreeable.

Jumilla

The vineyards of Jumilla, which lie inland from the Mediterranean port of Alicante, have been known since Roman times. Almost the whole production is of exceptionally full-bodied red wines with a high degree of alcohol. They can be drunk young.

Interesting wines are made throughout Spain, but many of them never come to Britain. Some of the finest red wines in the country come from the valley of the Duero, near Valladolid, in the newly classified area of Ribera del Duero. The wines are aged in cask for several years before bottling and achieve enormous fruit and flavour. Because the area is quite cool, the alcoholic degree is not too high.

PORTUGAL

The wines of Portugal have long been represented in Britain by port and little else. However, efforts have recently been made to introduce us to other wines of the country. Of these, the most successful has been *Vinho Verde*, which comes from vineyards in the north of the country, where the vines often grow high on trellises. Whilst the wines can be red or white, in Britain they are almost invariably white. They are low in alcohol, fairly high in acidity and with a slight sparkle. They make ideal summer drinking served chilled.

Dao, which is pronounced something like dung, makes some of Portugal's best red table wines. The vineyards lie inland to the south of the river Douro, on hard granitic soil. The wines tend to be rather tannic when young and benefit from ageing. The older qualities are described as *reserva*, or *garrafeira* when aged in bottle. They should be opened an hour or two before serving.

The commonest wines of Portugal however are their popular rosés, with slight sweetness and a slight, artificially induced sparkle. More interesting are the fresh red and white wines of *Bairrada* and the very pleasant white wine of *Bucelas*. For those with a sweet tooth, an old *Moscatel de Setubal* is one of the world's outstanding pudding wines.

Some of Austria's best known white wines come from the vines grown in these vineyards in Gumpoldskirchener.

AUSTRIA

For a small country, Austria produces a remarkable selection of wines. Many of them are in the German style and the same words will appear on the label. One of the most appealing is made from their native grape variety, the Grüner Veltliner, particularly from around the town of Falkenstein. It is an agreeable clean dry wine, with a hint of sweetness. Rather sweeter is *Schluck*, from the beautiful area of Wachau on the River Danube. Other towns well-known for their white wines are Gumpoldskirchener, just to the south of Vienna, and Krems to the north-west.

SWITZERLAND

Few of the country's wines find their way to export markets which is a pity. The best wines come from the steep hillsides on the northern shore of Lake Geneva. The predominant grape variety is the Chasselas, known locally as the Dorin. Here in the Canton of Vaud, there are a few small villages with a high reputation, such as Dézaley. Further to the east in the Valais, the Chasselas is called the Fendant and again makes fine white wines.

Some red wine is made in Switzerland from the Gamay and the Pinot Noir. The best is sold under the name of *Dole*.

HUNGARY

Historically, Hungary has based its wine reputation firmly on the wines of Tokay, one of the best sweet wines in the world. Nowadays the range is rather wider and there are dry Tokays, recognized by the word *szamorodni* on the label. Sweet wines are classified as *aszu* and by the number of *puttonyok* or tubs of the sweetest grapes added to each. The maximum is five. Even sweeter, and rarer, is *Essencia*, made from natural run juice from unpressed grapes. This can be one of the most expensive wines in the world.

On a much more down to earth level is the *Bull's Blood* from the town of Eger. This red wine ages more than it is generally allowed and can make an exceptional bottle when it is eight or more years years old. When drunk younger, *Bull's Blood* can seem rather rough.

Agreeable white wines are made from members of the Riesling family near Lake Balaton, and wines with rather more character come from the native Furmint grape.

YUGOSLAVIA

This has been the most successful of all the Eastern European countries in introducing its wines into the British market. Its spearhead has been the Riesling grape, though not the true Riesling of Germany but its Italian cousin called the Laski Riesling. The slightly sweet, soft wines have appealed to the consumer. Another wine to note is the *Ranina Radgona*, or 'Tiger's Milk', from the north-east of the country, which is rather richer.

The red wines have been rather less successful, but some excellent Cabernet Sauvignon is now being made. The best quality Yugoslavian wines come from the northern areas of Slovenia and Croatia.

BULGARIA

Of the other Eastern European countries, Bulgaria has recently shown that it is capable of making excellent single grape variety wines at reasonable prices. Amongst the most successful are the Cabernet Sauvignon, especially from Sakar Mountain, and the Merlot from Trakia. Of the white Bulgarian wines, the Sauvignons and the Chardonnays have the most appeal.

RUSSIA

This is now one of the most important wine-producing countries in the world—thanks to its campaign against the drinking of vodka—but its wines do not appeal much to British consumers. Sweetness seems to be a prerequisite with heaviness coming a close second. The best vineyards are in Georgia, where there is a great deal of emphasis on ports and champagnes, or their Russian equivalents.

THE UNITED STATES

Whilst wineries seem to be springing up all over the United States, the bulk of the vineyards for making wine—as opposed to grape jelly—are in California and New York State. The majority of the wines from New York are sweet with a peculiar taste that comes from the local native grapes. Some wineries are beginning to make classic wines in the European mould, but their production is very limited.

In California, however, a range of quality wines is made which could rival that of the whole of Europe. The reason for this is the enormous variety of climates in the one State ranging from the baking Central Valley to the cool Russian River area. Fine, dry autumns, and the possibility to irrigate encourage experimentation. The fact that owning vineyards has tax advantages has also meant that many wealthy men have sought the best techniques from around the world and been prepared to invest in them.

These advantages mean that very little bad wine is made in California. Some of it might not appeal to our tastes, but it is nearly always well made. Most European grape varieties are planted and they are often sold as single wines, or varietals. Of these, the best are probably the Cabernet Sauvignon for red wines and the Chardonnay for whites. However, there is an enormous variation in price.

Among the best wine-producing regions of California are the Napa and Sonoma Valleys to the north of San Francisco and Monterey County to the south. While the styles of the wines vary considerably, Californian wines often have a higher alcoholic degree and more concentration of flavour than their European equivalents.

ARGENTINA

This country has an important domestic consumption of wine—the third largest *per capita* in the world—and therefore much of the wine made is nothing more than *vino de*

Wine storage in vast, stainless steel tanks in a North American vineyard, where wine-making means mass production.

mesa. But some excellent wines are made from the best European varieties. The best vineyards are in irrigated semi-desert land in the province of Mendoza and the most successful variety is probably the Cabernet Sauvignon.

CHILE

The country of Chile is over 3,000 miles long and there are vineyards for almost a third of this length. The best wines, however, come from the Maipo Valley not far from the capital Santiago. There is a notable French tradition in viticulture and wine-making and the best wines probably come from the Bordeaux grape varieties: Cabernet Sauvignon, Merlot, Cabernet Franc and Cot for reds, and the Sauvignon for whites.

NORTH AFRICA

During the French colonial days, the vineyards of North Africa were of prime importance, for their rich, heavy wines, low in acidity, blended well with the thin French wines of the Midi. Now that blending of wines from outside the Common Market with those from within it is forbidden, the role of the vineyards of Algeria, Tunisia and Morocco has largely collapsed. Algeria, especially, now makes little quality wine. The situation has been accentuated because all three countries are Moslem and therefore opposed to alcohol in principle. Tunisia and Morocco have a pragmatic approach and make sound red and rosé wines.

SOUTH AFRICA

The first grapes were pressed for wine in South Africa as long ago as 1659 and exported to Holland and the East Indies within a very short time. In more recent times, there has been a concentration on making port- and sherry-style wines. It is only over the past few years that efforts have been made to make quality table wines.

In order to help the consumer, a series of 'stripes' has been introduced to guarantee the authenticity of the wines: a blue stripe gives the area of origin, a red stripe the year of harvest, a green stripe the grape variety. In addition, certain wines are awarded a 'superior' status and the word 'Estate' can only appear if the wine is bottled where it is produced.

Much stress is laid on varietal wines and several different grapes are grown. The following are native to South Africa:

Steen: also sometimes called the Chenin Blanc, though it is not the French grape of that name, but something rather closer to a Sauvignon. It makes white wines throughout the sweetness spectrum.

Riesling: again a South African variant. The true German Riesling is called the Weisser Riesling.

Pinotage: a cross between the Pinot Noir and the Cinsault. It gives an almost sweet red wine when young, but ages into a full-bodied, Rhône-style wine.

AUSTRALIA

The developments of wine-making in this country are so rapid that it is difficult to keep up with them. Wine is now made in all the States apart from the Northern Territories

A modern winery at Angle Vale, South Australia.

and whilst it might have been possible a few years ago to pinpoint the best regions, experimentation has shown that good wines can be made in a much wider range of places than previously thought.

Generally speaking the most fashionable area is the Hunter Valley, for this is on the doorstep of Sydney, the main centre of consumption. However, great wines are also made in the Swan Valley and Margaret River areas of western Australia, throughout the south-eastern part of South Australia (particularly Coonawarra for reds) and much of Victoria.

The most successful red wines use the Cabernet Sauvignon and the Shiraz (the Syrah of the Rhône Valley) grapes, while the best white wines are made from the Riesling, which is only rarely the true German Riesling, the Sémillon and the Chardonnay. Generic European names such as Claret and Burgundy are often used indiscriminately on the home market.

Another feature of the labelling of Australian wines is that of 'Bin Numbers'. Many growers will make a wine of a specific style each year which will be given a Bin Number. There will be a continuity of style through a succession of vintages, though there will of course be differences from year to year.

NEW ZEALAND

The making of fine wine on a commercial basis in New Zealand is much more recent and has really gathered pace only in the past fifteen years or so. Until then the bulk of production had been of fortified wines, mainly in the Auckland area. Many of the growers were immigrants from the Balkans, whose interests lay more in quantity and strength than quality.

Great advances are now being made and the most successful wines are probably made from German grape varieties, such as the Müller-Thurgau. White wines represent a significant majority of the production.

SPARKLING WINES

A sparkling wine conjures up a picture of festivity and it is perhaps because of this that several governments have decreed that higher taxes should be paid upon them. The wines tend to be more expensive anyway, for they have to be in stouter bottles to resist the pressure of the gas within; they must have bigger, tighter-fitting corks for the same reason; and the presentation is more lavish. The added production costs, too, can be substantial. But there is nothing magical about a sparkling wine—it can be a fun wine to drink on any occasion, not just on racecourses and at weddings and christenings.

A lovely summer view of the sweeping Champagne vineyards at Oger in the Côte des Blancs, south of Epernay.

I have already said that sparkling wine is made by letting the second fermentation take place in the bottle, but this is in fact the most expensive way of making it, known as the *méthode champenoise*.

The wine is bottled after the first fermentation and the bottles laid to rest so that the second fermentation takes place in the bottle. This creates a deposit, which must be removed before the wine can be sold. The traditional way of achieving this is to put the bottles in sloping racks and turn and shake the bottle a little each day so that ultimately they finish vertically upside down with the deposit on the corks. The necks of the bottles then pass through a freezing brine

The time-consuming job of turning the bottles (remuage) *in the cellars of Moët and Chandon in Epernay.*

solution, the deposit is ejected in a pellet of ice and the bottles topped up with wine and a cane sugar solution.

The most labour-intensive part of this operation is the shaking, or *remuage* as it is called. This is done by hand, with a man shaking a bottle in each hand at a time and working his way through thousands of bottles a day. As a process this lasts weeks.

Over the past few years, there have been certain innovations to speed up the process. Some companies now put the bottles on vast metal racks which can be moved as a whole. The latest advance is to have these racks controlled by computer programmes, so that the *remuage* can take place 24 hours a day, seven days a week. The whole process can thus be considerably shortened, saving both time and money, but the quality of the wine is not impaired.

The second, and now very common, method of making sparkling wine is by the *cuve close* or *Charmat* treatment. In this, the secondary fermentation takes place under pressure in vast stainless steel tanks. The wine is then drawn off and bottled, again under pressure. Thus the whole process of *remuage* is avoided and the process shortened from months, or even years, to a matter of weeks. Whilst there is no doubt that the best *méthode champenoise* wine will be better than the best *cuve close*, a good *cuve close* can be excellent.

The third production method is by simply carbonating a still wine, in the same way that you might make lemonade or tonic water, but this gives an unattractive end product, with large bubbles, and such wines are rarely seen.

CHAMPAGNE

The Champagne vineyards are amongst the most northerly in the world and have as their commercial centre the city of Reims, some 100 miles east of Paris. The countryside is rolling chalk-land and the vineyards are split into three areas: to the north the Montagne de Reims, where the Pinot Noir, a black grape-variety is grown; on the banks of the river Marne are the vineyards of the Vallée de la Marne; and stretching southwards from the other important town of the area, Épernay, are the vineyards of the Côte des Blancs, where the white grape, the Chardonnay grows.

Champagne is generally sold under a brand name, for the trade is dominated by a number of important companies such as Moët et Chandon, Veuve Clicquot, Krug and Bollinger. Some of these companies will have vineyards of their own but, at best, these only account for a small proportion of their total requirements. They will therefore buy grapes or, possibly, wine from the vast number of vineyard owners.

Champagne is almost always a blended wine and the ideal blend will probably include wines from the three vineyard areas. Each village in the Champagne vineyard region has a percentage classification and the price paid for the grapes from that village is calculated on this basis.

Whilst the large houses dominate the trade with their brands, a considerable amount of Champagne is also sold under the B.O.B. label (Buyer's Own Brand). Thus a major chain of stores, or even an individual restaurant, might sell a Champagne under its own label. The source can be traced from a producer's reference number on the label. A small amount may also be sold under the label of an individual grower.

Champagnes are generally classified by their style and sweetness, as described below. Of the various styles, non-vintage is by far the most important.

Non-vintage: produced from wine of more than one year. At the very heart of the business of any of the larger companies is the need to provide a Champagne of a certain quality that it can maintain from year to year. Thus it will continually strive to find a variety of base wines that go together to make the required end product. The quantities of fruit produced each year in Champagne vary considerably, for the region is at the limit of the vine, and the quality of each vintage will also be different. As the blender may well have to work towards a bottle which will not be sold for many years, his role is of great importance. In Champagne the fact that a wine does not bear a vintage is not important for the ideal non-vintage blend should be better than a wine from a single year.

Vintage: produced in a very good year when a firm decides to sell a wine from that particular year alone. Naturally the style will vary according to the year.

Rosé Champagne: is, as its name suggests, a pink Champagne. At present it seems to enjoy a certain vogue in Britain. The flavour tends to be rather fuller than a normal Champagne.

Crémant: this has a less aggressive sparkle than is normal. It is definitely for those who dislike bubbles going up their nose! (Although you will not come across it on the label, a *pétillant* wine is one with a gentle fizz.)

Blanc des Blancs: a white Champagne made solely from white grapes and is something of a speciality of the Côte des Blancs. It is often rather lighter in taste and has an agreeable delicacy.

Blanc des Noirs: a rarity. It is a white wine made just from the black Pinot Noir grape and is produced by only a small number of growers, largely on the Montagne de Reims where white grapes are not grown. The wine has a tendency to be rather full and unbalanced.

Coteaux Champenois: this is still wine from the Champagne region. More commonly it is white, but occasionally red. Generally it represents poor value for money. In a region that has deservedly built up its reputation on fine sparkling wines, still wines are rather an anti-climax.

Many companies also produce a *de-luxe* quality, under an impressive brand-name, and often in a special shaped bottle. They can be vintage or non-vintage wines. Basically they should represent the highest quality within the style of that particular company.

Champagne is also classified by its sweetness. Variations in this are achieved when the deposit is discharged from the bottle. As has already been said, this is replaced by a mixture of wine and cane sugar solution. The proportion of sugar added determines the final sweetness of the wine.

The driest classification is *brut* or sometimes Extra Dry. Theoretically this should have little or no sugar in the mixture, but slowly over the years *brut* wines seem to have become progressively less dry. As a result some companies have introduced such classifications as *brut sauvage* to designate a sugarless wine.

The next stage up is *sec*, meaning dry, but in effect meaning slightly sweet, then come *demi-sec* and *doux*. The last is unseen in Britain and is frighteningly sweet.

OTHER SPARKLING WINES

France. Most of the vineyard regions of France produce sparkling wines by the Champagne method. Perhaps the best are Crémant d'Alsace, Crémant de Bourgogne, Vouvray and Saumur from the Loire valley, and Blanquette de Limoux from the South of France. Lesser wines are produced in Gaillac, Seyssel and Saint-Péray.

Cuve close wines are also widely produced in France and are generally a satisfactory alternative for those who do not want to pay the price of a *méthode champenoise* wine.

Germany. Few of the host of German sparkling wines are made by the Champagne method, though there are several that are most enjoyable. The majority are made from a blend of German and imported wine and have a sweetness that appeals to the German palate. The finest, though even this includes a broad spectrum of qualities, is called *sekt*, which must have aged for a minimum of nine months in Germany. Next down the scale comes *schaumwein* and, well towards the bottom, is *perlwein* which is lightly gassed and often made on the Sodastream principle.

Italy. By far the majority of Italian sparkling wine is made by *cuve close*, including those great favourites *Lambrusco* and *Asti Spumante*. The first is red, slightly sparkling and generally sweet. It is low in alcohol and has become a great favourite with the novice American wine drinker. The second is white and sweet, often with a distinct flavour of the Moscato grape, rich and fruity.

Spain. Just south of Barcelona lies the area of Penedés, where Spain's finest sparkling wines are made by the Champagne method. They bear on the label the word *cava*. Codorníu and Freixenet are the two largest producers of sparkling wines in the Penedés area; between them they produce about seventy per cent of all the sparkling wine made in the region. Other well known firms making *cava* wines are Castellblanch, Conde de Caralt and Marqués de Monistrol. *Cava* wines are also produced to the north of Barcelona and by two firms in Rioja, one with some success the other with much less. They are refreshing wines with the long-lasting *méthode champenoise* bubble.

FORTIFIED WINES AND VERMOUTHS

In some countries, comparatively little wine is drunk with a meal; much of it may be taken just before, or after, food. But in Britain, there is a long tradition of certain wines being drunk at all times during the day. In Victorian times, for example, a glass of Madeira or Malaga might be taken for elevenses, or even instead of afternoon tea. Whilst these wines are now drunk much less here, sherries and ports have continued this long tradition.

Carefully terraced vines on the difficult hills of Duoro at Pinhão, centre of the port wine country.

Vermouths, which are basically wines flavoured with a variety of herbs, have also come to take an important place in the market. They have found many new consumers amongst those who have been accustomed to drinking spirits but who have decided to change, possibly as a result of ever increasing duties.

There are basically two ways of fortifying wines: to make sherry, for example, grape spirit is added to wines which have fermented out completely; but to make port, brandy is added before the fermentation has been completed, resulting in a sweeter wine, as the grape sugar will not have been converted into alcohol.

SHERRY

Sherry takes its name from the town of Jerez, in the south of Spain, some 60 miles south of Seville. It was already widely appreciated in Shakespearean times and was recognized as being a superior wine.

The finest sherry vineyards have soil rich in limestone and are blindingly white under the summer sun. The three main grape varieties of the region are the Palomino, the Pedro Ximenez and the Moscatel. The grapes are allowed to ferment out fully, but in the case of the Pedro Ximenez which are left to dry out in the sun, some sugar can be left.

When fermentation has taken place, the wines are tasted and classified according to their characteristics. The lighter wines will become *finos* and the more full-bodied *olorosos*. A form of fungus called *flor* appears on the surface of *fino* wines in the cask; its action accentuates the style of the wine and produces the delicate flavour.

As most sherry is sold under a brand name, it is essential that continuity of style be maintained over the years. In order to achieve this, the wine is 'brought up' by the *solera* system. In this there may be four or more 'classes' of casks with hundreds of casks in each 'class'. When the producer requires some wine, he draws off a proportion from each of the casks in the oldest class. These are then filled with wine from the previous class, and so on to the first class which will consist of the youngest wine in the *solera*. Sometimes one comes across a wine which might be labelled something like 'Solera 1868'. This does not mean that the wine in the bottle is of that vintage, but that the *solera* was laid down in that year. Theoretically, the system assures that there is a minute fraction of the original wine in the current blend, but it is the overall characteristic of the wine that is important.

Main Styles of Sherry

Fino: a very dry sherry, pale in colour and light in alcohol content.

Manzanilla: a *fino* sherry, made in Jerez and aged in the town of Sanlucar de Barrameda, which is on the estuary of the Guadalquivir river. *Manzanilla* is a trifle bitter and some say that it has a slightly salty taste reminiscent of the sea air.

Amontillado: this should be an aged *fino*. It will be amber in colour and have a round, dry, nutty taste. Generally sold as a medium sherry.

Palo Cortado: a full-bodied, but dry wine; somewhere between a *fino* and an *oloroso*.

Oloroso: a full-bodied wine, which can vary in colour and sweetness. It is used as the base wine for cream and brown sherry, but can also be found as a naturally dry wine. It tends to be higher in alcohol content than a *fino*.

Brown: this is an *oloroso* to which sweetening and colouring wine has been added. It is far less fashionable than it used to be.

Amoroso: similar to brown sherry, but generally more golden in colour and better quality.

Cream: this is an *oloroso* wine to which sweetening wine from the Pedro Ximenez grape has been added.

Pale Cream: this is a light, *fino* sherry which has had a sweetening wine added.

Other Types of Sherry

Sherry comes just from the Jerez region of Spain, but there are a number of similar wines made around the world. Of these perhaps the best also come from Spain, from the Montilla-Moriles region, south of Côrdoba. These wines are remarkably similar in style and have tended to be rather cheaper, because they are lower in alcohol and thus have a lower rate of duty.

Sadly, much of what passes for 'sherry' in the rest of the world is of inferior quality, though some excellent wines do come from South Africa, California and Cyprus. Generally speaking it is easier to make better wines in the sweeter styles. However, some countries have now managed to breed the *flor* fungus and produce reasonable dry wines.

The grapes are left out in the sun to concentrate the sugar for making sweet sherries.

PORT

This is the other great fortified wine. It takes its name from the city of Oporto in northern Portugal. Whilst there are no vineyards in the immediate neighbourhood, it is in that town that all the major companies are situated. The port vineyards begin some 50 miles up the valley of the river Douro, clinging precariously to the steep slate and granite hillsides of that river and its tributaries.

Sadly the days are long gone when Britain was the market that dominated the port trade. The wine was created by Britons for Britons and the trade people in Oporto are largely British, but it is now the French who are the largest consumers; sadly often of not very good wine.

Samuel Johnson described port as the liquor 'for men', but in Britain it has been partly preserved as a ladies drink— mixed with lemonade!

To make port, the fermentation is stopped by the addition of brandy. With rare exceptions port is always sweet. As recent drinking habits have meant a move towards drier wines, lower in alcohol, the sales of port have suffered. A fine port however, is still one of the great wines of the world.

Main Styles of Port

Ruby: this is the commonest style—full-bodied, rich and sweet.

Tawny: this is much lighter in colour and can be achieved in two ways. It can be a blend of young ruby and white wines, which create a wine similar to a *ruby*, but lacking some of its robustness; or it can be achieved by long ageing in the cask. This method produces a better *tawny*, which can become light in colour but browning slightly round the edge—you can see it in the glass— silky soft, with a lot of finesse. Occasionally, they can be found with an indication of age on them, such as 'Ten Years Old'. As a rule of thumb, the older the port the finer it is, though very old wines can be rather delicate.

White: this is golden rather than truly white and tends to be drier than other ports. It is recommended as an aperitif—though you may find it rather a heavy one.

Vintage: the finest wines selected in the best years. They are bottled when they are two years old and then stored for a minimum of ten years and perhaps as much as 50 or more before being drunk. In the bottle they throw a deposit which sticks to the side and is known as a 'crust'. They should be decanted before serving, so that none of the crust gets in the glass.

The Barco Rabelo was the sailing vessel traditionally used to transport the casks of port down the river Duoro.

Late bottled vintage or L.B.V.: these are wines of a particular vintage, bottled between four and six years old. They should be of high quality, full-bodied and very smooth. Normally they will not need further ageing, and should not need decanting.

Crusted: this is often an excellent alternative to *vintage* port. It has many of the same characteristics, though it is usually a blend of wines of a variety of vintages. It can be left to age, and should be decanted.

Vintage character: a top-quality, full-bodied, *ruby* port.

Other Types of Port

Other port-style wines are made in South Africa, Australia and California, though often the name has been abused and the result is a sweet wine, high in alcohol. Their strength has made them very attractive to a certain type of drinker.

However, I have tasted really superb old 'ports', from both Australia and California. Normally they can be recognized by the high price that is asked for them!

MADEIRA

The island of Madeira belongs to Portugal. It is some 400 miles off the coast of Morocco in the North Atlantic. The vineyards are very steep and the soil exceptionally rich. In order to maximize the production of the limited amount of land available, the vines are trained along trellises and vegetables grow underneath.

Madeira is another wine that was improved beyond measure as the result of an accident. As the wine was of poor quality, it was often sent out as ballast in ships sailing to the Indies. Someone tasted some on its return and decided that it was much more palatable than when it had set out.

As the cost of sending all the wine out to the tropics and back for improvement would be prohibitive, a trip simulator has been developed. The wine is put into vats or rooms which are gradually heated to a temperature of about 50°C (130°F) and left there for four or five months. These saunas are called *estufas*. The result is that the wine has been aged and softened more rapidly than is usual.

As with port, this sweet wine is created by adding brandy to grape juice which has not finished fermenting. To maintain continuity of character, the *solera* system operates as for sherry (see page 62).

There are four main grape varieties used in Madeira. They give their names to the wines, though it does not necessarily mean the wine is made just from that variety.

Types of Madeira

Sercial: is the driest. It is clean and crisp with some bite to it. It is rather fuller in body than a good *fino* sherry.

Verdelho: though dry, this has a distinct honey background and is ideal for those who like something soft but not sweet.

Bual: is sweet and supple, but not heavy and cloying.

Malvasia or *Malmsey*: is very full-bodied, rich-brown in colour, and with an enormous perfume. But it has the contrasting snap of acidity that is typical of all wines of Madeira.

OTHER FORTIFIED WINES

Marsala This is made in Sicily and again owes its origins to British needs for full-bodied wines to keep out the damp. Generally it is sweet, though it can be found in dry styles. It has a distinctive taste of burnt almonds. Much of its present-day role appears to be in the kitchen.

Malaga This comes from the south of Spain, to the east of Gibraltar. It is made from two grape varieties that give exceptionally sweet wines. The finest quality is Lágrima which is made solely from free-run juice—i.e., the grapes are not pressed at all. For those who like the taste of the Muscatel grape, the Moscatel Malaga is interesting; less so are their attempts at dry wines.

Pineau des Charentes A fortified wine of the Cognac brandy region of France, it is made in the same way as port, by adding brandy to grape juice. Generally it is a golden colour, but can also be found in a rosé style. It should be sweet, but with a very clean finish in the mouth. Similar wines are made on a small scale in Champagne (*ratafia*) and the Armagnac region (*floc*).

Vermouth The tradition of adding herbs to wine is almost as old as wine itself. There have been two main reasons for this: poor wine can often be made palatable, or be preserved longer, if herbs are added to it; the second is medicinal. For centuries the monasteries were the dispensaries to the sick. Each had its own herb-garden and a store of wine, which was needed for mass. It was therefore a natural progression that the goodness should be obtained from the herbs by infusing them in wine. With the coming of sugar from the Indies, and the widening use of distillation, these remedies became more palatable; spirit was substituted for wine and sugar added to mask the bitterness of many of the herbs.

Nowadays, vermouth is made mainly in Italy and France, though it is also produced in almost every other wine-making country. Italian vermouths tend to be sweeter than French. The base wines are generally of low quality, but this fact is masked by the addition of concentrated sweet grape juice, brandy and up to 30 herbs, spices, fruits, barks and roots. Each company has its own formula and style.

Secco (It.), *Sec* (Fr.): is normally a pale green-yellow and has an agreeable herbal flavour.

Bianco (It.), *Blanc* (Fr.): is clear white and very much sweeter.

Rosso (It.) *Rouge* (Fr.): is, strangely, not red at all, but brown in colour. I find it rather more restrained than the white, though still sweet and herbal.

BUYING WINE

For most of us there are two places where we buy wine: in
restaurant to drink there, and in a shop to take home.

More and more restaurant-owners are beginning to
realize that the sale of wine can be a very useful source of
income and are taking more care over the range of wine
they offer and the way they are presented.

When you are shown the menu, you should be given the
wine-list at the same time, for the food and wine should be
chosen together. Whilst it is often difficult to find the wine
that will match what everybody is eating, it is usually
possible to reach a happy compromise.

Although not the traditional place to buy wine, many supermarkets now offer excellent selections.

Do not be afraid of the wine-list, or the wine-waiter. If you do not understand something or are unsure as to what to order, ask his advice.

Many people prefer to stick to a wine they already know, but whilst this is playing safe, it might be a mistake. If you are completely lost for ideas, ask for the house wine—then at least if you have made a mistake it should not be an expensive one.

Before the waiter opens your bottle of wine, ask to see it, so that you can check that it is what you ordered. Far too often one finds that it is another vintage, another vineyard or another shipper. If you are not totally happy at this stage, send it back; if you ordered a lamb chop and were given a pork chop you wouldn't hesitate to return it, and the same should apply to wines. Sometimes you might be offered a better wine than you were expecting—but, from my experience, this does not often happen.

When the waiter has pulled out the cork, he should show it to you. You should then smell the end that has been in contact with the wine; if it smells of anything other than wine, the wine itself will probably be tainted. If the waiter asks you whether you want the wine decanting, accept his advice—he should know whether the wine would benefit from it or not.

As the person who has ordered the wine, you should be offered a little to taste first. There are two reasons for this: firstly, you can taste the wine to see whether it is satisfactory; and secondly, it means that any particles of cork that might have come from the action of the corkscrew will be in your glass and not that of your guest.

It is often advisable to smell your glass before anything is poured into it, as it can happen that it might have traces of detergent which would ruin the taste of the wine. By changing the glass, you can avoid an expensive mistake.

If at the tasting stage you are unhappy with the wine—you think it smells strange, is cloudy, or tastes terrible—do not hesitate to ask the wine-waiter to try it himself. If he agrees with you he will change the bottle without question. If he does not agree, still ask for it to be changed if you are convinced that it is faulty. This can happen and it is part of his job—he is paid to wait on you. However, please do not adopt the odious habit of a wealthy American I once met. As a matter of course, he always sent back at least one bottle of wine, just to impress the people that were eating with him.

When most people buy wine in a shop, they buy it for drinking in the very near future. Generally speaking, all supermarkets sell nothing but wines which are ready for drinking, so that is one problem you do not have to worry about. In a wine shop, you can generally ask the assistant or manager about this point.

There are certain basic facts, however, you should know about the wine you are intending to buy. Many of these will be on the label, which will often tell you what the vintage is and, in many cases, the style of the wine. But all this may be written in a foreign language and mean nothing to you. In the chapter on table wines I have given many of the phrases that might be found on the labels of a particular country or region. In addition, here is a brief glossary of words or phrases you might find on labels in a number of languages.

GLOSSARY OF TERMS

English	French	German	Spanish	Italian
Wine	Vin	Wein	Vino	Vino
Ordinary wine	Vin de Table	Tafelwein	Vino de Mesa	Vino da Tavola
Bottle	Bouteille	Flasche	Botella	Bottiglia
Dry	Sec or Brut	Trocken	Seco	Secco
Medium-sweet	Demi-sec	Halb-Trocken	Semi-seco	Amabile or Abboccato
Sweet	Doux	Süss	Dulce	Dolce
Red	Rouge	Rot	Tinto	Rosso or Nero
White	Blanc	Weiss	Blanco	Bianco
Rosé	Rosé	Schillerwein or Weissherbst	Rosado	Rosato
Deep rosé/ Light red	Clairet	Rötlich	Clarete	Chiaretto
Vintage	Millesime	Weinlese	Cosecha	Vendemmia
Sparkling	Mousseux	Sekt or Schaumwein	Espumoso	Spumante
Estate bottled	Mise en bouteille au château/ domaine	Eigener Abfüllung or Erzeuger-abfüllung	Embotellado de origen or Engaraffado de Origen	Imbottigliato nel'origine

VINTAGES

The fact that there is a vintage on the label is by no means a guarantee of quality, but there is no doubt that for the average wine-drinker it helps to see a date on the bottle.

In certain regions vintages are very rarely used, because it is taken for granted that the wine that you will be drinking comes from the last year's crop. Alternatively, if you come across a Champagne or a Port with a vintage date on it you can be sure that it comes from a very good year, because tradition has laid down that only such wines will be sold with a mention of the year.

Some people believe that the best wines are those sold as non-vintage, for the producer then has the opportunity of balancing out any extremes there might be of a particular vintage. This is what should happen with most Champagnes. However, there are two main problems. Firstly, if the bottle does not have a vintage date on it, it is difficult to know how old the wine is: it may not yet be ready for drinking, or it might well be way over the top.

The second problem is that in such regions as Bordeaux

GOOD VINTAGES
France
Red Bordeaux: (1986), (1985), (1983), (1982), 1981, 1979,
1978, 1975, 1973, 1970
Sweet white Bordeaux: (1986), (1983), 1976
Red Burgundy: (1985), (1983), 1982, 1979, 1978, 1976
White Burgundy: 1985, 1983, 1982, 1981, 1979, 1978
Beaujolais: 1985, 1983
Rhône: (1985), (1983), 1982, (1978)
Alsace: (1985), (1983), 1982, 1981, 1976

Germany
1985, 1983, 1981, 1980, 1979, 1976

Spain
Red Rioja: (1985), (1983), (1982), 1981, 1978

Italy
Northern Italian reds: (1985), 1983, (1982), 1979, 1978

Portugal
Port: (1985), (1983), (1982), (1980), (1977), 1975, 1970, 1966,
(1963)

and particularly Burgundy, where for climatic reasons there
might be considerable differences between the vintages,
some unscrupulous merchants use the Non-Vintage (or
VSR) label as a convenient melting-pot and disguise for
those vintages they would have difficulty in selling under
their true colours. Here again, it is a question of buying wine
from someone in whom you have trust.

Generally speaking, therefore, there is no point in looking
for a vintage on an ordinary wine, for it will have been
blended and released for immediate consumption. But if you
are paying for a better bottle of wine, it is better to have the
security of a vintage, as long as it is a good one.

The brief list above gives the better vintages for a small
number of regions. Where a year appears in brackets, this
indicates that you might have to wait some time before the
greatest wines of that year reach their peak. Any vintage
chart is nothing more than a guide and should be treated
with care. Even in the worst years some successful wines are
made and in the best there is always the possibility of a
failure. Just because a year has been omitted from my list
does not mean that all wines of that year are bad;
conversely, the fact that I give 1976 a good rating for
Burgundies by no way means that you can be guaranteed to
have an excellent bottle of wine whenever you choose it.

One of the most exciting developments in recent years has been the interest shown by supermarket chains in the selling of wine. With their vast buying power, they have been able to impose strict additional quality standards on the suppliers. In addition, their own labels often carry much information that would not have been on those of the supplier, and this will help the purchaser. Furthermore, some chains have moved up-market, now offer a range of the highest quality wines at good prices. Sometimes their buyers can achieve this as a result of having found excellent wines from the less fashionable vintages. Even the disadvantage of supermarket-buying—the fact that there are not trained assistants to advise on each wine—is now being remedied. In many areas, the supermarket chains have speakers available to talk to groups about their wines.

WINE FOR INVESTMENT

Over the past few years, several companies have specifically promoted wine for investment, but this is something that should be approached with extreme care. Much pleasure can be gained by buying wine young, financing the operation by selling part of it later at a healthy profit. On the other hand, there are some who speculate in wine as they might in any other commodity without the slightest thought of drinking any of the wine they have bought.

The main difference between wine and a number of the other commodities used as investment tools is that wine is a finite product. It is mortal; there is a time at which it reaches its peak—after that it can only decline in quality and value.

If you want to invest in wine, or even if you want to buy wine to celebrate a birth, but not to be drunk until the child's twenty-first birthday, it is essential to buy wines that will have a long and healthy life in front of them. For this I would only recommend vintage ports and red Bordeaux wines from the greatest years and the best *châteaux*.

One other thing I would say: never pay more for such a bottle of wine than you would if you knew that you were going to have to drink it yourself—there is always the possibility you might have to do just that!

WINE LABEL TERMS

The following annotations indicate the standard information to look for on a selection of typical wine labels.

① Vintage
② Château
③ Appellation controllée
④ Bottled at the château
⑤ Name of the producer
⑥ Content by volume
⑦ Country of production

① Name of producer
② Estate bottled
③ Vintage
④ Region
⑤ Village and vineyard
⑥ Grape variety and quality level of wi
⑦ Quality wine guarantee and certific
⑧ Content by volume (EEC standard)
⑨ Country of production

BODEGAS ALAVESAS, S.A.
Laguardia (Rioja Alavesa)

RIOJA
DENOMINACION DE ORIGEN CONTROLADA

SOLAR
DE
SAMANIEGO

COSECHA 1981

PRODUCED AND BOTTLED AT
BODEGAS ALAVESAS, S. A.

PRODUCE OF SPAIN

U. K. AGENTS
JMW LONDON W9

12,3 %   70 cl. e.

Name of the producer	⑤	Vintage
Region	⑥	Where bottled
Guarantee of controlled name	⑦	Alcohol content
Brand name	⑧	Content by volume

AZIENDA AGRICOLA
dei Conti
GUERRIERI-RIZZARDI

Valpolicella
Denominazione di Origine Controllata
V. Q. P. R. D.
Classico Superiore

0.750 lt.   12 % vol.

Imbottigliato all'origine dal viticoltore
Guerrieri Rizzardi - Bardolino
ITALIA

VINO NON PASTORIZZATO

Name of the producer	⑥	Where bottled
Name of the wine	⑦	Alcohol content
Guarantee of controlled name	⑧	Country of production
Sub-region and classification	⑨	Non-pastuerized wine
Content by volume		

STORING AND SERVING WINE

For most of us nowadays a cellar is a thing of the past. In France, every new house still seems to have one and even if you live in a block of flats you generally have your own portioned-off part of the basement. Even those fortunate enough in Britain to live in a house which has a cellar probably find that it is dominated by the central heating boiler. Where then can we store wine? Do we even need anywhere to store wine?

Port served with Stilton cheese is a classic combination and an excellent conclusion to a good meal.

The outlets where one can purchase wine are now much more numerous than in the past; many supermarkets, for example, now sell a much wider range of wines, including a limited number of great wines. These are all largely ready for drinking, so there is really much less necessity for wine to be stored at home. More wine for the home is now bought by women than men, so one must assume that much is bought only shortly before it is needed. It has become part of the regular weekly shopping. Nevertheless, many of us like to have some bottles of wine in reserve, perhaps for the unexpected guest, but lack the place to store them.

The traditional answer to this problem has often been

Store bottles on their sides, with labels uppermost and necks towards you for easy access.

beneath the stairs, but I am not convinced that this is the ideal place. Other answers may have been in the loft or the garage, but these, too, have certain drawbacks. What then are the requirements?

Basically, they are quite simple: lack of disturbance and a constant temperature. Ideally, the place should be quite cool, somewhere about 11°C (52°F), but what is more important is that it does not change too much. A cellar, where there is a boiler; under the stairs, where there is often some disturbance; or in a loft or a garage, where the temperature can fluctuate widely between winter and summer are therefore not ideal.

My particular answer has been to put my wine racks in a fitted cupboard in a room which is not often used. The cupboard is against an inside wall, and I do not have central heating in the room. The wines seem to keep quite well there, though as their turnover is quite rapid perhaps it is not a fair test! Most people must have a similar quiet spot in the house where bottles can be kept.

Wine should be stored with the bottles lying on their sides. If they are stored upright, the cork might dry out and the seams that occur in cork release a fine powder that will taint the wine. This does not happen if the end of the cork facing the wine is kept moist.

Racks are ideal for storing wine, as one bottle can be removed without disturbing the others. It is most sensible to have the bottles lying with the corks facing outwards and the labels upwards so that you can easily recognize the wine in the rack. Additionally, if a deposit has formed in the wine, you know on which side of the bottle it is and disturb it as little as possible when removing the bottle from the rack.

Opening the Bottle

When you open a bottle, cut the capsule back from the neck so that the metal does not come into contact with the wine.

when it is poured. Also wipe the neck of the bottle and the top of the cork with a clean cloth. Occasionally, there might be dirt or even mould on the top of the cork; do not worry, this will not have tainted the wine.

The choice of corkscrew is a very personal matter. I prefer one that has a very long screw, so that it can get to the bottom of the cork and eliminate the risk of leaving some of it behind in the bottle. I also prefer a corkscrew which operates by placing pressure on the bottle; you can then just continue turning it in the same direction to insert the screw and withdraw the cork. The best of these is the Screwpull, invented by a Texan space scientist. It costs more than an ordinary corkscrew, but is worth the difference just for the trouble avoided.

To open a bottle of sparkling wine, hold the bottle in one hand and put your other hand over the cork, with a cloth to avoid the possible risk of a cut. Turn the bottle against the cork—not the cork against the bottle. If you have difficulty in extracting the cork, it can be held with special pliers. If the top of the cork comes off in your hand, be careful when trying to get the rest out with a corkscrew. Champagne corks are so tight that you run a real risk of breaking the corkscrew!

One impressive, but often impracticable and always messy, alternative for dealing with a broken cork is to hold the bottle horizontally on a table and strike the neck of the bottle at the base of the cork a very firm blow from a heavy knife. With luck, the neck will break cleanly—and you will have Champagne all over the carpet!

One word of warning: whilst it is impressive to let a Champagne cork fly out when you open the bottle, it can also be very dangerous. A lost eye from a flying cork is something most people would prefer to avoid.

For the lover of the more unusual wine paraphernalia, here are some things called port tongs. I must admit I have never used them, but I think I understand the principle involved. As vintage port is often drunk when it is extremely old, it can happen that the cork will crumble at the approach of a corkscrew. This is the moment for the tongs. They are heated in the fire then applied as clamps to the neck of the bottle, which will crack and come away with the cork.

Decanting Wine

To decant or not? That is the equivalent question to members of the wine trade as that of the mediaeval philosophers when they tried to determine how many angels could dance on the head of a pin! My personal feeling is that

Decanting is worth the effort—very ordinary red wines, in particular, benefit from the exposure to air.

there are two very good reasons for decanting in certai circumstances. Firstly, if there is a deposit in the wine, it i much more satisfactory to know that you can pour ever drop of wine from your decanter and know that it will b star-bright, rather than to have to worry whether a guest wi get some deposit in his glass.

The second reason is perhaps more open to discussion. feel that there are certain wines which benefit fror exposure to air before being drunk: it helps them to open ou and become more attractive. Amongst these are the grea red wines of Bordeaux, old-style Riojas with some age, an some of the better Italian wines. This must be the result c the grape-varieties and the ageing and vinification techni ques used.

On the other hand, Burgundies are very rarely decanted i the region itself. Even if they have a deposit in the bottl they are generally served from a wine-basket, though thi demands a very steady hand.

Whilst decanting is not difficult, it does demand a certai amount of practice and preparation. First of all, you shoul take the bottle gently out of the rack and place it in wine-basket. Alternatively, if you do not have a basket, tak the bottle out some hours before you are going to decant an stand it upright, so that the deposit may fall to the bottom c the bottle.

Make sure your decanter is clean and not musty smellin which can happen if it is not used very often. Ideally, should be rinsed out with a little wine.

Find a source of bright light. Traditionally this has been a candle, but a torch with a narrow beam will work just as well. Open the bottle and take it firmly in one hand. Hold the decanter in the other hand. Pour steadily, with the light shining upwards on the neck of the bottle where the wine is pouring through. To start with you will see that the wine is bright, but towards the end of the bottle you will begin to see some of the deposit arriving. That is when you finish.

It is essential that all the pouring is done in one continuous motion, otherwise the deposit might be disturbed and you will either get it in the decanter and thus defeat the whole object of the exercise, or else you will find that you are having to reject too large a proportion of the bottle.

In no way is a deposit in a wine a fault—it is a natural occurrence in the ageing process. Wines can be treated so that they do not throw a deposit and this is generally done with most commercial wines of standard quality, by either chilling or pasteurising the wine, depending on its colour.

Sometimes a deposit can be seen in a white wine and some drinkers take the bottle back claiming it is out of condition. The deposit is a natural one of tartrate crystals which tend to form if the wine is chilled. It is not a sign of bad wine though neither is it, as some producers would try to make believe, a sign of a particularly good one either. Just pour gently!

Serving Wine

At what temperature should a wine be served? This is a matter of personal preference. There is a cliché that red wine should be served at room temperature, but I feel that this must date from the times when rooms were a great deal cooler than they are nowadays. Certainly there is little less pleasant than a bottle which has been put on the top of a stove or by the fire to bring it up to tepidity.

My personal feeling is that most red wines should be brought into the room where they are going to be drunk about four hours before the meal and opened about an hour before. However, I regularly serve Burgundies somewhat cooler. In any case, it is much easier to warm up the wine in a glass in your hand than it is to chill it!

There are even some red wines that taste better if they are slightly chilled. Beaujolais is one good example—its fruity taste is enhanced if it has spent an hour or so in the fridge.

A general rule for white wines is that sweeter wines should be served colder than drier ones. I tend to serve white Burgundies at cellar temperature (see page 78), but put most other white wines and sparklers in the fridge for an hour. Whilst the authorities do not recommend it, wine doe not seem to suffer from being placed in a freezer—though b certain to remember you've put it there or you might find lot of broken glass amongst your frozen peas!

I am not a fan of an ice-bucket as it tends to chill the win too dramatically and also leave the wine in the neck of th bottle at a totally different temperature, which means tha the first person to be served receives an unpleasant war glass of wine. To counter this you have to turn the bott upside down, rather inelegantly, to have all the wine at th same temperature.

What are the best wine glasses? Even now, every win area likes to design its own. I even have a friend who ha had a glass designed specially for sparkling wine fro Alsace. Whatever anyone may say, there is one ideal desig for a wine glass: a tulip shape, made of plain uncut cryst Red wine glasses should hold about 250 ml (8 fl oz), b should not be filled to more than a third. White wines shou be served in slightly smaller glasses, so that they do not los their chill while in the glass.

How should wine be served? Rather as has been outline on page 70, when talking about buying a wine in restaurant. The cork should be smelt and a little wine p into your own glass first, before you serve any to your guest

Basically wine is made to be drunk and most of the win that is made is certainly not in need of too much care in i presentation. But one of the attractions of wine must sure be that it can be enjoyed on a countless number of levels. a formal dinner party, it is worth taking the effort of servin the wine so that it shows at its best. A cheap wine will n suffer if it is made a fuss of, but an expensive one might if is not treated with the correct amount of care. Whilst much the ceremony appears nothing less than pretentious to th outsider, there is very good reason behind most of it.

Similarly, tasting of wine can appear stupid. However, ju a little effort is well rewarded—though it may not seem at elegant. To get the taste of a wine properly, put a little your mouth, lean forward, purse your lips and breathe through them. You will be surprised how much extra flavo you can get.

Some people worry that wine will be wasted if it is not drunk at once. With most wine you can put the cork back the bottle, put it in the fridge and finish it the ne day—some wines will even taste better. If for some reas the wine does not taste pleasant, still don't throw away—use it for cooking. A drop of wine will impro almost any dish.

WINE WITH FOOD

Wine and food are not things that can be treated separately, for one is generally made for the other. I say generally, for it is not always the case. The Germans, for example, frequently drink wine by itself and as a result the wines that they make are, for the most part, low in alcohol and slightly sweet. On the other hand, their close neighbours the Alsatians make, from the same grape varieties, wines that are dry and much higher in alcohol. That is because the Alsatian is a wine-with-meal drinker. This does not mean that you should not drink German wines with food, but it is often more difficult to find the perfect match.

In most parts of the World local wines match local foods. Thus in Italy and Spain, where a lot of oil is used in cooking, the ordinary wines are often high in acidity. This acidity is an antidote to the oil and they balance each other out. Such wines are never meant to be drunk by themselves, and if you were to try one without food you would find it extremely rough. On the other hand it is not always right to take the local wine with the local food specialities.

A lot of writers have said that there are certain rules one should respect when drinking wine with food. In 'The Plain Man's Guide to Wine', Raymond Postgate attempts to summarize the necessary minimum knowledge about wine on a postcard. He begins: 'Don't serve red wine with fish' and ends 'Follow your own taste not others'. To me the two concepts might well be contradictory.

An interesting combination worth trying: Gewürztraminer d'Alsace and smoked salmon.

Indeed, this might often happen in a restaurant when a[l] in a party but one are eating meat and the last is havin[g] fish—many will not buy a separate wine for the singleton. [I] have frequently drunk red wine with fish in such circum[-] stances and enjoyed it—though I probably would hav[e] enjoyed a white wine rather more.

Wine is made to be enjoyed, so when choosing a wine t[o] accompany a meal, choose one that you will enjoy. Most c[f] us tend to be rather conservative and when we have found [a] wine we like, we often stick with it. But there is no doub[t] that there are ideal combinations between certain foods an[d] certain wines, and we should be bold enough to try them. [A] historical one in Britain is Stilton cheese and vintage port.

It is also true that certain foods do not go at all well wit[h] wines, such as dishes which involve eggs or chocolate an[d] even salads. To put up a fine wine with these is to ask for [a] massacre—and an expensive one at that.

There are also certain dishes which I find to be bette[r] matched by drinks other than wine; for example, India[n] food is admirably suited to beer. There are some who like t[o] take a full-bodied rosé wine with it, but this is generall[y] swamped. I also find it very difficult to match a wine t[o] smoked fish in any form. However, a glass of good aquavit o[r] schnapps . . .

Apart from the relationship between wine and food whe[n] one is enjoyed with the other, there is also the importan[t] relationship of one being an ingredient of the other. Ther[e] can be few recipes which are not improved by the additio[n] of wine: a simple consommé is transformed by a glass of dr[y] sherry or Madeira; a stew benefits from some red wine in th[e] sauce, even if it is only the dregs from last night's bottle; [a] little vermouth in the gravy with your Sunday roast por[k] will give it a delightful herbal flavour. The possibilities ar[e] endless and a little experimentation is always rewarded.

It can be interesting and instructive to analyse the taste [of] any wines that you might taste at home or in a restauran[t] and make a note of them. For example, it is not difficult t[o] recognize whether a wine is dry or sweet, or whether it has [a] lot of acidity. In red wines, something else that can b[e] recognized is whether a wine has tannin—this is a[n] important factor if you are buying a wine to keep, for it give[s] it its 'backbone'. If your teeth and tongue get a furry coatin[g] when you taste a wine, it is most probably tannin, and th[e] wine will improve.

Whilst there are words that the professionals use t[o] describe the characteristics of a wine—and the meaning o[f] these is usually self-evident—do not hesitate to use you[r]

Pears in red wine: one way of using wine as an ingredient in cooking rather than just as an accompaniment to a meal.

own words and associations to fix a wine in your mind. It will make buying wine in the future much more easy.

One final use for wine: as a preventative, or restorative, medicine. One firm of wine shippers in London used to give every member of staff a glass of port every winter's morning—and there was no absenteeism because of colds or flu. I can speak from experience as to the dramatic effect a raw egg beaten up in a glass of port can give a tired body!

WHAT TO DRINK WITH WHAT

Drink what you like with whatever you want but,
White wine is better with fish and red wine is better with red meat.
Better food demands better wine. Cheaper food does not suffer from better wine.
* *If you are having more than one wine with your meal start with the driest and finish with the sweetest.*
* *Similarly, begin with the lightest-bodied wine and finish with the fullest-bodied.*

Bearing all this in mind, I have compiled the following chart of the sorts of wines that accompany a number of different dishes and drinking occasions. Most of them can be easily obtained from high street supermarkets, wine merchants, and off-licences. For the white, rosé and sparkling wines, I have also given a sweetness classification from (1) Very Dry to (9) Very Sweet. Thus, for certain dishes, I may have given a number of wines of varying sweetness.

You can then select the one you want according to personal taste, always remembering that if you are going to have another wine later in the meal, it is better if the first one is drier.

The wines have been split into three price classifications. These are not tied to a specific money limit, but rather to the importance of the meal. Thus:

★ *An ordinary everyday wine, for an ordinary meal.*
★★ *A better wine, but one which should not dent the family budget too much.*
★★★ *A special wine, for the special occasion, whatever it might be.*

After each wine, I have also put a simple code to show its colour and the country and region it comes from. Thus, if you cannot find the actual wine mentioned in your shop, you know approximately what to look for. Thus a Châteauneuf-du-Pape appears as R-F-Rh=Red, French, Rhône. (An explanation of the various letters appears opposite.)

SPECIAL OCCASIONS	★
Picnic	*Soave W-I-V (2)* *Vinho Verde W-P-VV (4)* *Valpolicella R-I-V* *Rosé d'Anjou Re-F-L (4)*
Christening/Wedding	
Cheese and Wine Party	*All Bag in Box wines* *Orvieto Secco W-I-U (2)* *Grüner Veltliner W-A-LA (3)* *Laski Riesling W-Y-SI (4)* *Coteaux du Tricastin R-F-Rh* *Valdepeñas R-S-Va* *Chiaretto di Bardolino Re-I-V (2*
Bottle Party	*Vin de France Dry W-F (1)* *Vin de France Medium Dry W-* *Hock Deutscher Tafelwein W-G* *Lambrusco Grasparossa di* *Castelvetro RSpg-I-ER*
Barbecue	*Corsican Red R-F-Co*
Indian Food (Beer or . . . .)	*Rosé d'Anjou Re-F-L (4)*
Chinese Food	*Soave W-I-V (2)* *Morio-Muskat W-G (4)*
Drinking without Food	*Piesporter Michelsberg W-G-M* *Bergerac Rouge R-F-Bc* *Portuguese Rosé Re-P (4)*

KEY TO FOLLOWING TABLES

COLOUR/STYLE			
R Red		Rh Rhône	S Spain
Re Rosé	G	Germany	Ju Jumilla
Spg Sparkling		M Mosel	Pe Penedes
W White		N Nahe	Ra Rioja
		Pf Pfalz	Va Valdepeñas
		Rhg Rheingau	Val Valencia
COUNTRY/REGION		Rhh Rheinhessen	US United States
A Austria	I	Italy	C California
Bu Burgenland		ER Emilia Romagna	Y Yugoslavia
LA Lower Austria		Fr Friuli	Sl Slovenia
F France		Pi Piedmont	
Al Alsace		TM The Marches	
Bc Bergerac		Ty Tuscany	
Bs Beaujolais		U Umbria	
Bx Bordeaux		V Veneto	
By Burgundy	P	Portugal	
Ch Champagne		D Dao	
L Loire		Ma Madeira	
LR Languedoc-Roussilon		Pt Port	
Pr Provence		VV Vinho Verde	

	★★★
...hlener Munzlay W-G-M (3)	Sancerre les Perriers W-F-L (1)
...aujolais R-F-Bs	Ch. de Poncie, Fleurie R-F-Bs
...lifornian Rose Re-US-C (4)	
...va Spanish Sparkling Spg-S-Pe (2)	Champagne Spg-F-Ch (1)
...o Spumante Spg-I-Pi (6)	
...imur Spk-F-L (1)	
...penheimer Krötenbrunnen	
...G-Rhh (5)	
...nt Emilion R-F-Bx	
... de Gourgazaud, Minervois	
...-LR	
...sé de Provence Re-F-Pr	Tavel Rosé Re-F-Rh
...vaner d'Alsace W-F-Al (2)	
...desheimer Rosengarten W-G-N (4)	Erdener Treppchen Auslese
...e de Brouilly R-F-Bs	W-G-M (7)
...bernet Rosé d'Anjou Re-F-L (4)	Moulin Touchain Anjou 1964 W-F-L (7)

THE MEAL	★
Aperitif	Manzanilla Pale Dry S (1)
	Montilla Dry S (1)
	Amontillado Sherry S (2)
STARTERS	★
Consommé	Amontillado Sherry S (4)
	Fino Sherry S (2)
Smoked Fish (Aquavit or . . .)	
Prawn Cocktail	Orvieto Secco W-I-U (2)
Oysters (Guinness or . . .)	Muscadet de Sèvre et Maine W-F-L (1)
Mussels	Blanc de Blancs du Val de Loire
	Saumur W-F-L (1)
	Rioja Seco Viña Castil W-S-Ra (
Charcuterie, Pâté, Cold meats	Soave W-I-V (2)
	Côtes du Ventoux R-F-Rh
Melon (Ogen)	
Avocado Pear	Blanc Anjou W-F-L (4)
	Bornheimer Trappenberg W-G-
FISH	★
Coarse Fish	Côtes du Roussillon W-F-LR (1)
	Sauvignon Vin de Pays de Loir
	Cher W-F-L (1)
Salmon, Trout—poached or grilled	Grüner Veltliner W-A-LA (3)
Salmon, Trout—in sauce	
Sole, Turbot—poached or grilled	
Sole, Turbot—in sauce	Orvieto Secco W-I-U (2)
	Rüdesheimer Rosengarten W-G-N (4)
Crab, Lobster	Bordeaux Blanc Medium Dry W-F-Bx (4)
	Bornheimer Trappenberg W-G
PASTA	★
	Soave W-I-V (2)
	Riesling-Italico W-I (4)
	Barbera del Monferrato R-I-Pi

	★★★
ıi Friulano di Aquileia W-I-Fr (1)	
ınur Méthode Champenoise -F-L (1)	

	★★★
	Sercial Madeira P-Ma (2)
ʋurztraminer d'Alsace W-F-Al (2)	
łornian Pinot Chardonnay ∥S-C (2)	Deidesheimer Hergottsacker Kabinett W-G-Pf (4)
Tertre du Moulin, Entre Deux s W-F-Bx (1)	Chablis le Cru W-F-By (1)
	Domaine de la Bizolière Savennières W-F-L (1)
ırgogne Aligoté W-F-By (1) ːaner d'Alsace W-F-Al (2) ujolais R-F-Bs	
ʂcat d'Alsace W-F-Al (2)	Muscat de Beaumes de Venise W-F-Rh (9)

	★★★
ırgogne Aligoté W-F-By (1) ∘t Blanc d'Alsace W-F-Al (2) łicchio di Castelli di Jesi ∙TM (2)	
łing d'Alsace W-F-A (2) ːon Blanc Villages W-F-By (2) łornian Pinot Chardonnay ∥S-C (2)	Pouilly-Fumé W-F-L (2) Meursault W-F-By (2)
ʌtagny W-F-By (2)	Pouilly-Fuissé W-F-By (2) Ch. des Bidaudières, Vouvray W-F-L (4)
Tertre du Moulin, Entre Deux ᵃs W-F-Bx (1)	Puligny Montrachet W-F-By (2)
	Kiedricher Heiligenstock Kabinett W-G-Rhg (5)
ʐes-Hermitage W-F-Rh (2)	Corton-Charmlemagne W-F-By (2)

	★★★
ıi Friulano di Aquileia W-I-Fr (1)	

MEAT	★
Stews and Pies	*Minervois R-F-LR* *Coteaux du Tricastin R-F-Rh* *Jumilla R-S-Ju*
Grills	*Bergerac Rouge R-F-Bc* *Bordeaux Supérieur R-F-Bx*
Roast Lamb	*Barbera del Monferrato R-I-Pi* *Bordeaux Supérieur R-F-Bx*
Roast Pork	*Côtes du Ventoux R-F-Rh* *Bergerac Rouge R-F-Bc*
Roast Beef	*Dão R-P-D* *Coteaux du Tricastin R-F-Rh*
Chicken, Turkey—Roast	*Rioja Seco W-S-Ra (2)* *Piesporter Michelsberg W-G-M* *Laski Riesling W-Y-Sl (4)* *Niersteiner Gütes Domtal W-G-* *(4)* *Bordeaux Supérieur R-F-Bx*
Chicken-in sauce	*Riesling Italico W-I (4)* *Niersteiner Gütes Domtal W-G-* *(4)* *Blanc Anjou W-F-L (4)*
Game	*Coteaux du Tricastin R-F-Rh* *Corsican Red R-F-Co* *Barbera del Monferrato R-I Pi*

DESSERTS	★
Sorbet, Ice cream	*Moscatel de Valencia W-S-Val (8*
Pastry and light sweet puddings	*Premières Côtes de Bordeaux* *W-F-Bx (8)*
Christmas Pudding	*Vin de France, Sweet W-F (8)*
Fruit	
Exotic fruit	
Nuts	

CHEESE	★
Mild: Camembert, Brie	*Bergerac R-F-Bc*
Medium: Farmhouse Cheddar	*Côtes du Ventoux R-F-Rh*
Strong: Stilton, Roquefort	*Minervois R-Fr-LR*

	★★★
s-Hermitage R-F-Rh	Châteauneuf-du-Pape R-F-Rh
nes de Venise-Côtes du Rhône	Domaine Gigondas R-F-Rh
h	
ti Classico R-I-Ty	Ch. Tour des Combes, Saint Emilion
ilion R-F-Bx	R-F-Bx
ogne Rouge R-F-By	Ch. Giscours, Margaux, R-F-Bx
c R-F-Bx	Beaune Premier Cru R-F-By
Borie, Côtes du Rhône R-F-Rh	
u Bousquet, Côtes de Bourg	Domaine du Colombier, Chinon
x	R-F-L
ti Classico R-I-Ty	Ch. de Poncié, Fleurie R-F-Bs
o R-I-Pi	Ch. Cissac Haut-Médoc R-F-Bx
du Rhône Villages R-F-Rh	Ch. Grand Puy Ducasse, Pauillac
rnian Zinfandel R-US-C	R-F-Bx
	Gevrey-Chambertin R-F-By
ner d'Alsace W-F-A1 (2)	Puligny-Montrachet W-F-By (2)
rnian Chardonnay W-US-C (2)	
c R-F-Bx	Ch. Barreyres, Haut-Medoc R-F-Bx
es Bidaudières Vouvray	Deidesheimer Herrgottsacker
(4)	Kabinett W-G-Pf (5)
nes de Venise, Côtes du Rhône	Gevrey-Chambertin R-F-By
h	Gigondas R-F-Rh
	Domaine André Brunel, Châteauneuf
	du Pape R-F-Rh

	★★★
	Muscat de Beaumes de Venise
	W-F-Rh (9)
umante Spg-I-Pi (7)	Moulin Touchais Anjou W-F-L (7)
ne de la Soucherie, Coteaux	Apetloner Gewurztraminer
on W-F-L (7)	Beerenauslese W-A-Bu (9)
azillac W-F-Bc (7)	Sauternes W-F-Bx (8)
	Old Tawny Port R-P-Pt (8)
Beaulieu, Coteaux du Layon	Moulin Touchais, Anjou W-F-L (7)
(7)	
rztraminer d'Alsace W-F-A1	Uerziger Würzgarten Auslese
	W-G-M (7)
Sherry S (8)	Vintage Character Port R-P-Pt (8)
	Malmsey Madeira W-P-Ma (8)

	★★★
Gourgazaud, Minervois	Ch. Tourteau-Chollet, Graves R-F-Bx
R	
Borie, Côtes du Rhône R-F-Rh	Beaune R-F-By
	Ch. Giscours, Margaux R-F-Bx
rnian Zinfandel R-US-C	Châteauneuf-du-Pape R-F-Rh
	Vintage Port R-P-Pt (8)

FINDING OUT MORE ABOUT WINE

If this book has succeeded in interesting you in wine, how do you find out more about it? There are perhaps four main ways and the first of these is the most important—by drinking more of it!

To taste a wide range of wines is not always easy and can be expensive unless you can find others to share the cost. One way is to visit a wine-bar. There now appears to be at least one in every town of any size and most of them offer a range of wines by the glass. In this way you can taste three or four wines for what would normally be the price of a bottle.

Alternatively, if you have friends who are similarly interested, you could get together regularly and each bring a bottle of a specific range of wines. It is always instructional to taste wines of the same year, or perhaps made from the same grape variety, to see what differences there might be.

This can be carried a stage further by joining a wine society. These exist at all levels, from those for newcomers to wine to those which specialize in the wines of one region.

For further instruction, many Local Education Authorities now run evening classes in wine appreciation and it might be worth contacting them to see if they run one—and if they do not, whether they would be prepared to do so if there was sufficient demand.

If you are in any way—even remotely—connected with the wine-trade (perhaps you work in a restaurant) it is worth contacting the Wine and Spirit Education Trust, as they run series of lectures on wine at all levels in a number of venues around the country. Unfortunately, however, they are unable to cater for the general public.

There are an increasing number of magazines about wine, the oldest of which is *Decanter*, published monthly. This contains articles on wine in all its aspects, comparative tasting notes, and regular supplements about specific subjects, such as the wines of Spain. It is now widely read and respected around the world. It is, or should be, available from popular bookshops and newsagents.

On a less ambitious scale is *Which? Wine Monthly*, published by the Consumers' Association in the form of a newsletter, it usually contains a comparative tasting, notes on particular bargains available around the country and useful snippets of information. More recent is *What Wine?* which again lays particular stress on comparative tastings to find value-for-money wines.

The number of books on wine is large—and seems to be

increasingly rapidly. A useful book is George Rainbird's *An Illustrated Guide to Wine* (Octopus). Good paperbacks are available in Penguin and Faber. Also in a convenient format are the pocket-books produced by a number of publishers. The best-known of these is probably the *Pocket Wine Guide* by Hugh Johnson, who is always an interesting and informative writer. Another interesting writer is Jancis Robinson, who presented the 'Wine Programme' on the television.

Apart from drinking and reading, what more can be done to learn about wine? One answer is to visit the vineyards. There are now quite a few dotted about the south of England and many of them are happy to welcome visitors. Abroad, too, growers are generally most hospitable, but whilst some companies encourage tourists, with regular guided visits, there are many who have no more facilities than an open cellar door—and a limited knowledge of English. Your local wine-merchant may be able to fix you up with some useful addresses.

I hope this little book has done something to whet your appetite for the next bottle of wine. The exciting thing about the subject is that there is always more to learn and more bottles to open. As a notable 18th-century doctor once wrote: 'I know of nothing that springs from the earth so immensely diversified in its nature as wine.' Here's a health to that diversity!

Useful addresses:

Decanter Magazine, 2 St. John's Road, London SW11 1PN.

Which? Wine Monthly, Consumers' Association,
     Castlemead, Gascoyne Way, Hertford SG14 1LH.

What Wine? 55 Heath Road, Twickenham, Middlesex TW1
     4AW.

Wine Development Board (for general information on wine),
     5 Kings House, Kennet Wharf Lane, Upper Thames
     Street, London EC4V 3BH.

INDEX

ACKNOWLEDGEMENTS

The following photographs were taken especially for
Octopus Books:
Michael Boys 4, 9, 10, 43, 54-5; Colin Maher 16-7, 22, 24; Duncan
McNichol 76-7, 78, 83, 85; Tessa Musgrave 68-9; Octopus Books 63;
Jon Wyand 6-7, 41.
The publishers would like to thank the following organisations and
individuals for their kind permission to reproduce the photographs
in this book:
Patrick Eagar 13, 26-7, 52-3; Robert Estall 38, 51; John Freeman 80;
Picturepoint 14, 31, 48, 60-1; Topham Picture Library 33, 56; Zefa
Picture Library 2-3, 28, 34-5, 36, 46, 65.

Maps by Berry Fallon Design. Cartoons by Julia Whatley.